THE CAMBRIDGE MISCELLANY

II

MARLBOROUGH
AND OTHER POEMS

T0352287

MARLBOROUGH
and
OTHER POEMS

BY

CHARLES HAMILTON
SORLEY

CAMBRIDGE
AT THE UNIVERSITY PRESS
1932

CAMBRIDGE UNIVERSITY PRESS
Cambridge, New York, Melbourne, Madrid, Cape Town,
Singapore, São Paulo, Delhi, Tokyo, Mexico City

Cambridge University Press
The Edinburgh Building, Cambridge CB2 8RU, UK

Published in the United States of America by Cambridge University Press, New York

www.cambridge.org
Information on this title: www.cambridge.org/9781107651739

First published 1932
First paperback edition 2011

A catalogue record for this publication is available from the British Library

ISBN 978-1-107-65173-9 Paperback

PREFACE

The call for a new edition of these poems gives an opportunity for issuing them in a form which is intended to be definitive.

They are now arranged in four groups according to subject. It is true that all of them perhaps might be described by the title of one of these groups, as poems of life and thought. But some owe their inspiration directly to nature—to the wind-swept downs which the author loved and which he looked upon as "wise" as well as "wide"; a few reflect the experiences of school life; yet others show how his spirit faced the great adventure of war and death. Within each group the poems are printed, as nearly as may be, in the order of their composition, the title-poem being restored to its proper chronological place. When the date, exact or approximate, is known, it has been given; in those cases in which the date specifies the day of the month, it has been taken from the author's manuscript.

A single piece of imaginative prose is included amongst the poems. Other passages of prose were added to the third edition with the view of illustrating ideas occurring in the poems and prominent in the author's mind. With the exception of a few sentences from an early essay, these prose passages are all taken from familiar letters. To the present edition a few notes have been appended, in which some topical allusions are explained and what is known about the origin of the separate pieces is told.

The frontispiece is from a drawing in chalks by Mr Cecil Jameson.

Of the author personally, and of what he was to his family and his friends, I do not speak. Yet I may quote the phrase used by a German lady in whose house he had been living for three months. "The time with him," she wrote, "was like a holiday and a feast-day." Many have felt what she put into words: though it was the graver moods of his mind that, for the most part, sought expression in his poems. I may also put on record here the main facts concerning his short life.

He was born at Old Aberdeen on 19th May 1895. His father was then a professor in the University of Aberdeen, and he was of Scottish descent on both sides. From 1900 onwards his home was in Cambridge. He was educated at Marlborough College, which he entered in September 1908 and left in December 1913, after obtaining a scholarship at University College, Oxford. Owing to the war he never went into residence at the University. After leaving school he spent a little more than six months in Germany, first at Schwerin in Mecklenburg and afterwards, for the summer session, at the University of Jena. He was on a walking tour on the banks of the Moselle when the European war broke out. He was put in prison at Trier on the 2nd August, but released the same night with orders to leave the country. After some adventures he reached home on the 6th, and at once applied for a commission in the army. He was gazetted Second Lieutenant in the Seventh (Service) Battalion of the Suffolk Regiment before the end of the month, Lieutenant in November, and Captain in the following August. He was sent to France with his battalion on 30th May 1915, and served for some months in the trenches round Ploegsteert. Shortly after he had entered upon his life there, a suggestion was made to him about printing a slim volume of verse. But he put the suggestion aside as premature. "Besides," he added, "this is no time for oliveyards and vineyards, more especially of the small-holdings type. For three years or the duration of the war, let be." Four months later his warfare was accomplished. His battalion was moved south to take part in the battle of Loos, and he fell on 13th October 1915, in an attack in which the "hair-pin" trench near Hulluch was captured by his company. "Being made perfect in a little while, he fulfilled long years."

W. R. S.

CAMBRIDGE, *March* 1919

The Fifth Edition is an exact reprint of the Fourth Edition except for a few verbal changes on pages 58 and 60. These changes are due to the recovery, after nearly six years, of some of the author's manuscripts which he had left behind him in Germany in August 1914.

W. R. S.

CONTENTS

OF THE DOWNS

OF SCHOOL

OF LIFE AND THOUGHT

OF WAR AND DEATH

OF THE DOWNS

I

BARBURY CAMP

WE burrowed night and day with tools of lead,
Heaped the bank up and cast it in a ring
And hurled the earth above. And Caesar said,
"Why, it is excellent. I like the thing."
We, who are dead,
Made it, and wrought, and Caesar liked the thing.

And here we strove, and here we felt each vein
Ice-bound, each limb fast-frozen, all night long.
And here we held communion with the rain
That lashed us into manhood with its thong,
Cleansing through pain.
And the wind visited us and made us strong.

Up from around us, numbers without name,
Strong men and naked, vast, on either hand
Pressing us in, they came. And the wind came
And bitter rain, turning grey all the land.
That was our game,
To fight with men and storms, and it was grand.

For many days we fought them, and our sweat
Watered the grass, making it spring up green,
Blooming for us. And, if the wind was wet,
Our blood wetted the wind, making it keen
With the hatred
And wrath and courage that our blood had been.

So, fighting men and winds and tempests, hot
With joy and hate and battle-lust, we fell
Where we fought. And God said, "Killed at last
    then? What!
Ye that are too strong for heaven, too clean for hell,
(God said) stir not.
This be your heaven, or, if ye will, your hell."

So again we fight and wrestle, and again
Hurl the earth up and cast it in a ring.
But when the wind comes up, driving the rain
(Each rain-drop a fiery steed), and the mists rolling
Up from the plain,
This wild procession, this impetuous thing,

Hold us amazed. We mount the wind-cars, then
Whip up the steeds and drive through all the world,
Searching to find somewhere some brethren,
Sons of the winds and waters of the world.
We, who were men,
Have sought, and found no men in all this world.

Wind, that has blown here always ceaselessly,
Bringing, if any man can understand,
Might to the mighty, freedom to the free;
Wind, that has caught us, cleansed us, made us
    grand,
Wind that is we
(We that were men)—make men in all this land,

That so may live and wrestle and hate that when
They fall at last exultant, as we fell,
And come to God, God may say, "Do you come then
Mildly enquiring, is it heaven or hell?
Why! Ye were men!
Back to your winds and rains. Be these your heaven
    and hell!"

24 *March* 1913

II

STONES

THIS field is almost white with stones
   That cumber all its thirsty crust.
And underneath, I know, are bones,
   And all around is death and dust.

And if you love a livelier hue—
   O, if you love the youth of year,
When all is clean and green and new,
   Depart. There is no summer here.

Albeit, to me there lingers yet
   In this forbidding stony dress
The impotent and dim regret
   For some forgotten restlessness.

Dumb, imperceptibly astir,
   These relics of an ancient race,
These men, in whom the dead bones were
   Still fortifying their resting-place.

6

Their field of life was white with stones;
  Good fruit to earth they never brought.
O, in these bleached and buried bones
  Was neither love nor faith nor thought.

But like the wind in this bleak place,
  Bitter and bleak and sharp they grew,
And bitterly they ran their race,
  A brutal, bad, unkindly crew:

Souls like the dry earth, hearts like stone,
  Brains like that barren bramble-tree:
Stern, sterile, senseless, mute, unknown—
  But bold, O, bolder far than we!

14 *July* 1913

III

EAST KENNET CHURCH AT EVENING

I STOOD amongst the corn, and watched
   The evening coming down.
The rising vale was like a queen,
   And the dim church her crown.

Crown-like it stood against the hills.
   Its form was passing fair.
I almost saw the tribes go up
   To offer incense there.

And far below the long vale stretched.
   As a sleeper she did seem
That after some brief restlessness
   Has now begun to dream.

(All day the wakefulness of men,
   Their lives and labours brief,
Have broken her long troubled sleep.
   Now, evening brings relief.)

8

There was no motion there, nor sound.
    She did not seem to rise.
Yet was she wrapping herself in
    Her grey of night-disguise.

For now no church nor tree nor fold
    Was visible to me:
Only that fading into one
    Which God must sometimes see.

No coloured glory streaked the sky
    To mark the sinking sun.
There was no redness in the west
    To tell that day was done.

Only, the greyness of the eve
    Grew fuller than before.
And, in its fulness, it made one
    Of what had once been more.

There was much beauty in that sight
    That man must not long see.
God dropped the kindly veil of night
    Between its end and me.

24 *July* 1913

IV

AUTUMN DAWN

AND this is morning. Would you think
That this was the morning, when the land
Is full of heavy eyes that blink
Half-opened, and the tall trees stand
Too tired to shake away the drops
Of passing night that cling around
Their branches and weigh down their tops:
And the grey sky leans on the ground?
The thrush sings once or twice, but stops
Affrighted by the silent sound.
The sheep, scarce moving, munches, moans.
The slow herd mumbles, thick with phlegm.
The grey road-mender, hacking stones,
Is now become as one of them.
Old mother Earth has rubbed her eyes
And stayed, so senseless, lying down.
Old mother is too tired to rise
And lay aside her grey nightgown,
And come with singing and with strength
In loud exuberance of day,
Swift-darting. She is tired at length,
Done up, past bearing, you would say.

She'll come no more in lust of strife,
In hedge's leap, and wild bird's cries,
In winds that cut you like a knife,
In days of laughter and swift skies,
That palpably pulsate with life,
With life that kills, with life that dies.
But in a morning such as this
Is neither life nor death to see,
Only that state which some call bliss,
Grey hopeless immortality.
Earth is at length bedrid. She is
Supinest of the things that be:
And stilly, heavy with long years,
Brings forth such days in dumb regret,
Immortal days, that rise in tears,
And cannot, though they strive to, set.

*　　*　　*　　*　　*　　*　　*

The mists do move. The wind takes breath.
The sun appeareth over there,
And with red fingers hasteneth
From Earth's grey bed the clothes to tear,
And strike the heavy mist's dank tent.
And Earth uprises with a sigh.
She is astir. She is not spent.
And yet she lives and yet can die.
The grey road-mender from the ditch
Looks up. He has not looked before.
The stunted tree sways like the witch
It was: 'tis living witch once more.

The winds are washen. In the deep
Dew of the morn they've washed. The skies
Are changing dress. The clumsy sheep
Bound, and earth's many bosoms rise,
And earth's green tresses spring and leap
About her brow. The earth has eyes,
The earth has voice, the earth has breath,
As o'er the land and through the air,
With wingéd sandals, Life and Death
Speed hand in hand—that winsome pair!

16 *September* 1913

V

RETURN

STILL stand the downs so wise and wide?
  Still shake the trees their tresses grey?
I thought their beauty might have died
  Since I had been away.

I might have known the things I love,
  The winds, the flocking birds' full cry,
The trees that toss, the downs that move,
  Were longer things than I.

Lo, earth that bows before the wind,
  With wild green children overgrown,
And all her bosoms, many-whinned,
  Receive me as their own.

The birds are hushed and fled: the cows
  Have ceased at last to make long moan.
They only think to browse and browse
  Until the night is grown.

The wind is stiller than it was,
　　And dumbness holds the closing day.
The earth says not a word, because
　　It has no word to say.

The dear soft grasses under foot
　　Are silent to the listening ear.
Yet beauty never can be mute,
　　And some will always hear.

18 *September* 1913

VI

RICHARD JEFFERIES

(LIDDINGTON CASTLE)

I SEE the vision of the Vale
    Rise teeming to the rampart Down,
The fields and, far below, the pale
    Red-roofédness of Swindon town.

But though I see all things remote,
    I cannot see them with the eyes
With which ere now the man from Coate
    Looked down and wondered and was wise.

He knew the healing balm of night,
    The strong and sweeping joy of day,
The sensible and dear delight
    Of life, the pity of decay.

And many wondrous words he wrote,
    And something good to man he showed,
About the entering in of Coate,
    There, on the dusty Swindon road.

19 *September* 1913

VII

J. B.

THERE's still a horse on Granham hill,
And still the Kennet moves, and still
Four Miler sways and is not still.
    But where is her interpreter?

The downs are blown into dismay,
The stunted trees seem all astray,
Looking for someone clad in grey
    And carrying a golf-club thing;

Who, them when he had lived among,
Gave them what they desired, a tongue.
Their words he gave them to be sung
    Perhaps were few, but they were true.

The trees, the downs, on either hand,
Still stand, as he said they would stand.
But look, the rain in all the land
    Makes all things dim with tears of him.

And recently the Kennet croons,
And winds are playing widowed tunes.
—He has not left our "toun o' touns,"
    But taken it away with him!

October 1913

VIII

THE OTHER WISE MAN

(SCENE: *A valley with a wood on one side and a road running up to a distant hill: as it might be, the valley to the east of West Woods, that runs up to Oare Hill, only much larger.* TIME: *Autumn. Four wise men are marching hillward along the road.*)

ONE WISE MAN

I wonder where the valley ends?
On, comrades, on.

ANOTHER WISE MAN

    The rain-red road,
Still shining sinuously, bends
Leagues upwards.

A THIRD WISE MAN

    To the hill, O friends,
To seek the star that once has glowed
Before us; turning not to right
Nor left, nor backward once looking.
Till we have clomb—and with the night
We see the King.

ALL THE WISE MEN

The King! The King!

THE THIRD WISE MAN

Long is the road but—

A FOURTH WISE MAN

Brother, see,
There, to the left, a very aisle
Composed of every sort of tree—

THE FIRST WISE MAN

Still onward—

THE FOURTH WISE MAN

Oak and beech and birch,
Like a church, but homelier than church,
The black trunks for its walls of tile;
Its roof, old leaves; its floor, beech nuts;
The squirrels its congregation—

THE SECOND WISE MAN

Tuts!
For still we journey—

THE FOURTH WISE MAN

But the sun weaves
A water-web across the grass,
Binding their tops. You must not pass
The water cobweb.

18

The Third Wise Man

Hush! I say.
Onward and upward till the day—

The Fourth Wise Man

Brother, that tree has crimson leaves.
You'll never see its like again.
Don't miss it. Look, it's bright with rain—

The First Wise Man

O prating tongue. On, on.

The Fourth Wise Man

And there
A toad-stool, nay, a goblin stool.
No toad sat on a thing so fair.
Wait, while I pluck—and there's—and here's
A whole ring...what?...berries?

(*The Fourth Wise Man drops behind, botanizing.*)

The Wisest of the remaining Three Wise Men

O fool!
Fool, fallen in this vale of tears.
His hand had touched the plough: his eyes
Looked back: no more with us, his peers,
He'll climb the hill and front the skies
And see the Star, the King, the Prize.

But we, the seekers, we who see
Beyond the mists of transiency—
Our feet down in the valley still
Are set, our eyes are on the hill.
Last night the star of God has shone,
And so we journey, up and on,
With courage clad, with swiftness shod,
All thoughts of earth behind us cast,
Until we see the lights of God,
—And what will be the crown at last?

ALL THREE WISE MEN

On, on.

(*They pass on: it is already evening when the Other Wise Man limps along the road, still botanizing.*)

THE OTHER WISE MAN

A vale of tears, they said!
A valley made of woes and fears,
To be passed by with muffled head
Quickly. I have not seen the tears,
Unless they take the rain for tears,
And certainly the place is wet.
Rain-laden leaves are ever licking
Your cheeks and hands...I can't get on.
There's a toad-stool that wants picking.
There, just there, a little up,
What strange things to look upon
With pink hood and orange cup!

And there are acorns, yellow—green...
They said the King was at the end.
They must have been
Wrong. For here, here, I intend
To search for him, for surely here
Are all the wares of the old year,
And all the beauty and bright prize,
And all God's colours meetly showed,
Green for the grass, blue for the skies,
Red for the rain upon the road;
And anything you like for trees,
But chiefly yellow, brown and gold,
Because the year is growing old
And loves to paint her children these.
I tried to follow...but, what do you think?
The mushrooms here are pink!
And there's old clover with black polls,
Black-headed clover, black as coals,
And toad-stools, sleek as ink!
And there are such heaps of little turns
Off the road, wet with old rain:
Each little vegetable lane
Of moss and old decaying ferns,
Beautiful in decay,
Snatching a beauty from whatever may
Be their lot, dark-red and luscious: till there pass'd
Over the many-coloured earth a grey
Film. It was evening coming down at last.
And all things hid their faces, covering up
Their peak or hood or bonnet or bright cup

In greyness, and the beauty faded fast,
With all the many-coloured coat of day.
Then I looked up, and lo! the sunset sky
Had taken the beauty from the autumn earth.
Such colour, O such colour, could not die.
The trees stood black against such revelry
Of lemon-gold and purple and crimson dye.
And even as the trees, so I
Stood still and worshipped, though by evening's
    birth
I should have capped the hills and seen the King.
The King? The King?
I must be miles away from my journey's end;
The others must be now nearing
The summit, glad. By now they wend
Their way far, far, ahead, no doubt.
I wonder if they've reached the end.
If they have, I have not heard them shout.

  1 *December* 1913

IX

MARLBOROUGH

I

CROUCHED where the open upland billows down
　　Into the valley where the river flows,
She is as any other country town,
　　That little lives or marks or hears or knows.

And she can teach but little.　She has not
　　The wonder and the surging and the roar
Of striving cities.　Only things forgot
　　That once were beautiful, but now no more,

Has she to give us.　Yet to one or two
　　She first brought knowledge, and it was for her
To open first our eyes, until we knew
　　How great, immeasurably great, we were.

I, who have walked along her downs in dreams,
　　And known her tenderness, and felt her might,
And sometimes by her meadows and her streams
　　Have drunk deep-storied secrets of delight,

Have had my moments there, when I have been
　　Unwittingly aware of something more,
Some beautiful aspect, that I had seen
　　With mute unspeculative eyes before;

Have had my times, when, though the earth did wear
    Her self-same trees and grasses, I could see
The revelation that is always there,
    But somehow is not always clear to me.

II

So, long ago, one halted on his way
    And sent his company and cattle on;
His caravans trooped darkling far away
    Into the night, and he was left alone.

And he was left alone. And, lo, a man
    There wrestled with him till the break of day.
The brook was silent and the night was wan.
    And when the dawn was come, he passed away.

The sinew of the hollow of his thigh
    Was shrunken, as he wrestled there alone.
The brook was silent, but the dawn was nigh.
    The stranger named him Israel and was gone.

And the sun rose on Jacob; and he knew
    That he was no more Jacob, but had grown
A more immortal vaster spirit, who
    Had seen God face to face, and still lived on.

The plain that seemed to stretch away to God,
 The brook that saw and heard and knew no fear,
Were now the self-same soul as he who stood
 And waited for his brother to draw near.

For God had wrestled with him, and was gone.
 He looked around, and only God remained.
The dawn, the desert, he and God were one.
 —And Esau came to meet him, travel-stained.

III

So, there, when sunset made the downs look new
 And earth gave up her colours to the sky,
And far away the little city grew
 Half into sight, new-visioned was my eye.

I, who have lived, and trod her lovely earth,
 Raced with her winds and listened to her birds,
Have cared but little for their worldly worth
 Nor sought to put my passion into words.

But now it's different; and I have no rest
 Because my hand must search, dissect and spell
The beauty that is better not expressed,
 The thing that all can feel, but none can tell.

1 *March* 1914

X

LE REVENANT

HE trod the oft-remembered lane
  (Now smaller-seeming than before
  When first he left his father's door
For newer things), but still quite plain

(Though half-benighted now) upstood
  Old landmarks, ghosts across the lane
  That brought the Bygone back again:
Shorn haystacks and the rooky wood;

The guide post, too, which once he clomb
  To read the figures: fourteen miles
  To Swindon, four to Clinton Stiles,
And only half a mile to home:

And far away the one homestead, where—
  Behind the day now not quite set
  So that he saw in silhouette
Its chimneys still stand black and bare—

He noticed that the trees were not
  So big as when he journeyed last
  That way. For greatly now he passed
Striding above the hedges, hot

With hopings, as he passed by where
  A lamp before him glanced and stayed
  Across his path, so that his shade
Seemed like a giant's moving there.

The dullness of the sunken sun
  He marked not, nor how dark it grew,
  Nor that strange flapping bird that flew
Above: he thought but of the One....

He topped the crest and crossed the fence,
  Noticed the garden that it grew
  As erst, noticed the hen-house too
(The kennel had been altered since).

It seemed so unchanged and so still.
  (Could it but be the past arisen
  For one short night from out of prison?)
He reached the big-bowed window-sill,

Lifted the window sash with care,
  Then, gaily throwing aside the blind,
  Shouted. It was a shock to find
That he was not remembered there.

At once he felt not all his pain,
  But murmuringly apologised,
  Turned, once more sought the undersized
Blown trees, and the long lanky lane,

Wondering and pondering on, past where
  A lamp before him glanced and stayed
  Across his path, so that his shade
Seemed like a giant's moving there.

XI

LOST

Across my past imaginings
   Has dropped a blindness silent and slow
My eye is bent on other things
   Than those it once did see and know.

I may not think on those dear lands
   (O far away and long ago!)
Where the old battered signpost stands
   And silently the four roads go

East, west, south and north,
   And the cold winter winds do blow.
And what the evening will bring forth
   Is not for me nor you to know.

December 1914

OF SCHOOL

XII

RAIN

WHEN the rain is coming down,
And all Court is still and bare,
And the leaves fall wrinkled, brown,
Through the kindly winter air,
And in tattered flannels I
'Sweat' beneath a tearful sky,
And the sky is dim and grey,
And the rain is coming down,
And I wander far away
From the little red-capped town:
There is something in the rain
That would bid me to remain:
There is something in the wind
That would whisper, "Leave behind
All this land of time and rules,
Land of bells and early schools.
Latin, Greek and College food
Do you precious little good.
Leave them: if you would be free
Follow, follow, after me!"

When I reach 'Four Miler's' height,
And I look abroad again
On the skies of dirty white
And the drifting veil of rain,
And the bunch of scattered hedge
Dimly swaying on the edge,
And the endless stretch of downs
Clad in green and silver gowns;
There is something in their dress
Of bleak barren ugliness,
That would whisper, "You have read
Of a land of light and glory:
But believe not what is said.
'Tis a kingdom bleak and hoary,
Where the winds and tempests call
And the rain sweeps over all.
Heed not what the preachers say
Of a good land far away.
Here's a better land and kind
And it is not far to find."

Therefore, when we rise and sing
Of a distant land, so fine,
Where the bells for ever ring,
And the suns for ever shine:
Singing loud and singing grand,
Of a happy far-off land,
O! I smile to hear the song,
For I know that they are wrong,

That the happy land and gay
Is not very far away,
And that I can get there soon
Any rainy afternoon.

And when summer comes again,
And the downs are dimpling green,
And the air is free from rain,
And the clouds no longer seen:
Then I know that they have gone
To find a new camp further on,
Where there is no shining sun
To throw light on what is done,
Where the summer can't intrude
On the fort where winter stood:
   —Only blown and drenching grasses,
   Only rain that never passes,
   Moving mists and sweeping wind,
   And I follow them behind!

October 1912

XIII

A TALE OF TWO CAREERS

I SUCCESS

HE does not dress as other men,
  His 'kish' is loud and gay,
His 'side' is as the 'side' of ten
  Because his 'barnes' are grey.

His head has swollen to a size
  Beyond the proper size for heads,
He metaphorically buys
  The ground on which he treads.

Before his face of haughty grace
  The ordinary mortal cowers:
A 'forty-cap' has put the chap
  Into another world from ours.

The funny little world that lies
  'Twixt High Street and the Mound
Is just a swarm of buzzing flies
  That aimlessly go round:

If one is stronger in the limb
　　Or better able to work hard,
It's quite amusing to watch him
　　Ascending heavenward.

But if one cannot work or play
　　(Who loves the better part too well),
It's really sad to see the lad
　　Retained compulsorily in hell.

II FAILURE

We are the wasters, who have no
　　Hope in this world here, neither fame,
Because we cannot collar low
　　Nor write a strange dead tongue the same
As strange dead men did long ago.

We are the weary, who begin
　　The race with joy, but early fail,
Because we do not care to win
　　A race that goes not to the frail
And humble: only the proud come in.

We are the shadow-forms, who pass
　　Unheeded hence from work and play.
We are to-day, but like the grass
　　That to-day is, we pass away;
And no one stops to say 'Alas!'

37

Though we have little, all we have
   We give our School. And no return
We can expect for what we gave;
   No joys; only a summons stern,
"Depart, for others entrance crave!"

As soon as she can clearly prove
   That from us is no hope of gain,
Because we only bring her love
   And cannot bring her strength or brain,
She tells us, "Go: it is enough."

She turns us out at seventeen,
   We may not know her any more,
And all our life with her has been
   A life of seeing others score,
While we sink lower and are mean.

We have seen others reap success
   Full-measure. None has come to us.
Our life has been one failure. Yes,
   But does not God prefer it thus?
God does not also praise success.

And for each failure that we meet,
   And for each place we drop behind,
Each toil that holds our aching feet,
   Each star we seek and never find,
God, knowing, gives us comfort meet.

The School we care for has not cared
　　To cherish nor keep our names to be
Memorials.　God hath prepared
　　Some better thing for us, for we
His hopes have known, His failures shared.

November 1912

XIV

WHAT YOU WILL

O COME and see, it's such a sight,
So many boys all doing right:
To see them underneath the yoke,
Blindfolded by the elder folk,
Move at a most impressive rate
Along the way that is called straight.
O, it is comforting to know
They're in the way they ought to go.
But don't you think it's far more gay
To see them slowly leave the way
And limp and loose themselves and fall?
O, that's the nicest thing of all.
I love to see this sight, for then
I know they are becoming men,
And they are tiring of the shrine
Where things are really not divine.

I do not know if it seems brave
The youthful spirit to enslave,
And hedge about, lest it should grow.
I don't know if it's better so
In the long end. I only know

That when I have a son of mine,
He shan't be made to droop and pine,
Bound down and forced by rule and rod
To serve a God who is no God.
But I'll put custom on the shelf
And make him find his God himself.
Perhaps he'll find him in a tree,
Some hollow trunk, where you can see.
Perhaps the daisies in the sod
Will open out and show him God.
Or will he meet him in the roar
Of breakers as they beat the shore?
Or in the spiky stars that shine?
Or in the rain (where I found mine)?
Or in the city's giant moan?
   —A God who will be all his own,
   To whom he can address a prayer
   And love him, for he is so fair,
   And see with eyes that are not dim
   And build a temple meet for him.

30 *June* 1913

OF LIFE AND THOUGHT

XV

A CALL TO ACTION

I

A THOUSAND years have passed away,
 Cast back your glances on the scene,
Compare this England of to-day
 With England as she once has been.

Fast beat the pulse of living then:
 The hum of movement, throb of war
The rushing mighty sound of men
 Reverberated loud and far.

They girt their loins up and they trod
 The path of danger, rough and high;
For Action, Action was their god,
 "Be up and doing" was their cry.

A thousand years have passed away;
 The sands of life are running low;
The world is sleeping out her day;
 The day is dying—be it so.

A thousand years have passed amain;
  The sands of life are running thin;
Thought is our leader—Thought is vain;
  Speech is our goddess—Speech is sin.

II

It needs no thought to understand,
  No speech to tell, nor sight to see
That there has come upon our land
  The curse of Inactivity.

We do not see the vital point
  That 'tis the eighth, most deadly, sin
To wail, "The world is out of joint"—
  And not attempt to put it in.

We see the swollen stream of crime
  Flow hourly past us, thick and wide;
We gaze with interest for a time,
  And pass by on the other side.

We see the tide of human sin
  Rush roaring past our very door,
And scarcely one man plunges in
  To drag the drowning to the shore.

We, dull and dreamy, stand and blink,
    Forgetting glory, strength and pride,
Half—listless watchers on the brink,
    Half—ruined victims of the tide.

III

We question, answer, make defence,
    We sneer, we scoff, we criticize,
We wail and moan our decadence,
    Enquire, investigate, surmise;

We preach and prattle, peer and pry
    And fit together two and two:
We ponder, argue, shout, swear, lie—
    We will not, for we cannot, DO.

Pale puny soldiers of the pen,
    Absorbed in this your inky strife,
Act as of old, when men were men,
    England herself and life yet life.

October 1912

XVI

PEACE

THERE is silence in the evening when the long days
    cease,
And a million men are praying for an ultimate
    release
From strife and sweat and sorrow—they are praying
    for peace.
       But God is marching on.

Peace for a people that is striving to be free!
Peace for the children of the wild wet sea!
Peace for the seekers of the promised land—do we
       Want peace when God has none?

We pray for rest and beauty that we know we
    cannot earn,
And ever are we asking for a honey-sweet return;
But God will make it bitter, make it bitter, till we
    learn
       That with tears the race is run.

And did not Jesus perish to bring to men, not peace,
But a sword, a sword for battle and a sword that
    should not cease?
Two thousand years have passed us. Do we still
    want peace
        Where the sword of Christ has shone?

Yes, Christ perished to present us with a sword,
That strife should be our portion and more strife
    our reward,
For toil and tribulation and the glory of the Lord
        And the sword of Christ are one.

If you want to know the beauty of the thing called
    rest,
Go, get it from the poets, who will tell you it is best
(And their words are sweet as honey) to lie flat upon
    your chest
        And sleep till life is gone.

I know that there is beauty where the low streams
    run,
And the weeping of the willows and the big sunk
    sun,
But I know my work is doing and it never shall be
    done,
        Though I march for ages on.

Wild is the tumult of the long grey street,
O, is it never silent from the tramping of their feet?
Here, Jesus, is Thy triumph, and here the world's
    defeat,
        For from here all peace has gone.

There's a stranger thing than beauty in the ceaseless
    city's breast,
In the throbbing of its fever—and the wind is in the
    west,
And the rain is driving forward where there is no
    rest,
        For the Lord is marching on.

December 1912

50

XVII

THE RIVER

HE watched the river running black
  Beneath the blacker sky;
It did not pause upon its track
  Of silent instancy;
It did not hasten, nor was slack,
  But still went gliding by.

It was so black. There was no wind
  Its patience to defy.
It was not that the man had sinned,
  Or that he wished to die.
Only the wide and silent tide
  Went slowly sweeping by.

The mass of blackness moving down
  Filled full of dreams the eye;
The lights of all the lighted town
  Upon its breast did lie;
The tall black trees were upside down
  In the river phantasy.

He had an envy for its black
    Inscrutability;
He felt impatiently the lack
    Of that great law whereby
The river never travels back
    But still goes gliding by;

But still goes gliding by, nor clings
    To passing things that die,
Nor shows the secrets that it brings
    From its strange source on high.
And he felt "We are two living things
    And the weaker one is I."

He saw the town, that living stack
    Piled up against the sky.
He saw the river running black
    On, on and on: O, why
Could he not move along his track
    With such consistency?

He had a yearning for the strength
    That comes of unity:
The union of one soul at length
    With its twin-soul to lie:
To be a part of one great strength
    That moves and cannot die.

*   *   *   *   *   *

He watched the river running black
    Beneath the blacker sky.
He pulled his coat about his back,
    He did not strive nor cry.
He put his foot upon the track
    That still went gliding by.

The thing that never travels back
    Received him silently.
And there was left no shred, no wrack
    To show the reason why:
Only the river running black
    Beneath the blacker sky.

February 1913

XVIII

THE SEEKERS

THE gates are open on the road
That leads to beauty and to God.

Perhaps the gates are not so fair,
Nor quite so bright as once they were,
When God Himself on earth did stand
And gave to Abraham His hand
And led him to a better land.

For lo! the unclean walk therein,
And those that have been soiled with sin.
The publican and harlot pass
Along: they do not stain its grass.
In it the needy has his share,
In it the foolish do not err.
Yes, spurned and fool and sinner stray
Along the highway and the way.

And what if all its ways are trod
By those whom sin brings near to God?
This journey soon will make them clean:
Their faith is greater than their sin.

For still they travel slowly by
Beneath the promise of the sky,
Scorned and rejected utterly;
Unhonoured; things of little worth
Upon the highroads of this earth;
Afflicted, destitute and weak:
Nor find the beauty that they seek,
The God they set their trust upon:
—Yet still they march rejoicing on.

March 1913

XIX

ROOKS

THERE, where the rusty iron lies,
    The rooks are cawing all the day.
Perhaps no man, until he dies,
    Will understand them, what they say.

The evening makes the sky like clay.
    The slow wind waits for night to rise.
The world is half-content. But they

Still trouble all the trees with cries,
    That know, and cannot put away,
The yearning to the soul that flies
    From day to night, from night to day.

21 *June* 1913

XX

ROOKS (II)

THERE is such cry in all these birds,
    More than can ever be express'd;
If I should put it into words,
    You would agree it were not best
    To wake such wonder from its rest.

But since to-night the world is still
    And only they and I astir,
We are united, will to will,
    By bondage tighter, tenderer
    Than any lovers ever were.

And if, of too much labouring,
    All that I see around should die
(There is such sleep in each green thing,
    Such weariness in all the sky),
    We would live on, these birds and I.

Yet how? since everything must pass
    At evening with the sinking sun,
And Christ is gone, and Barabbas,
    Judas and Jesus, gone, clean gone,
    Then how shall I live on?

Yet surely Judas must have heard
    Amidst his torments the long cry
Of some lone Israelitish bird,
    And on it, ere he came to die,
    Thrown all his spirit's agony.

And that immortal cry which welled
    For Judas, ever afterwards
Passion on passion still has swelled
    And sweetened: so to-night these birds
    Will take my words, will take my words,

And wrapping them in music meet
    Will sing their spirit through the sky,
Strange and unsatisfied and sweet:
    That, when stock-dead am I, am I,
    O, that can never die!

25 *July* 1913

XXI

THE SONG OF THE UNGIRT RUNNERS

We swing ungirded hips,
And lightened are our eyes,
The rain is on our lips,
We do not run for prize.
We know not whom we trust
Nor whitherward we fare,
But we run because we must
  Through the great wide air.

The waters of the seas
Are troubled as by storm.
The tempest strips the trees
And does not leave them warm.
Does the tearing tempest pause?
Do the tree-tops ask it why?
So we run without a cause
  'Neath the big bare sky.

The rain is on our lips,
We do not run for prize.
But the storm the water whips
And the wave howls to the skies.
The winds arise and strike it
And scatter it like sand,
And we run because we like it
  Through the broad bright land.

XXII

GERMAN RAIN

THE heat came down and sapped away my powers.
The laden heat came down and drowsed my brain,
Till through the weight of overcoming hours
      I felt the rain.

Then suddenly I saw what more to see
I never thought: old things renewed, retrieved.
The rain that fell in England fell on me,
      And I believed.

XXIII

BRAND

THOU trod'st the shifting sand path where man's
    race is.
The print of thy soft sandals is still clear.
I too have trodden it those prints a-near,
But the sea washes out my tired foot-traces.
And all that thou hast healed and holpen here
I yearned to heal and help and wipe the tear
Away. But still I trod unpeopled spaces.
I had no twelve to follow my pure paces.
For I had thy misgivings and thy fear,
Thy crown of scorn, thy suffering's sharp spear,
Thy hopes, thy longings—only not thy dear
Love (for my crying love would no man hear),
Thy will to love, but not thy love's sweet graces,
That deep firm foothold which no sea erases.
I think that thou wast I in bygone places
In an intense eliminated year.
Now born again in days that are more drear
I wander unfulfilled: and see strange faces.

XXIV

PEER GYNT

When he was young and beautiful and bold
We hated him, for he was very strong.
But when he came back home again, quite old,
And wounded too, we could not hate him long.

For kingliness and conquest pranced he forth
Like some high-stepping charger bright with foam.
And south he strode and east and west and north
With need of crowns and never need of home.

Enraged we heard high tidings of his strength
And cursed his long forgetfulness. We swore
That should he come back home some eve at length,
We would deny him, we would bar the door!

And then he came. The sound of those tired feet!
And all our home and all our hearts are his,
Where bitterness, grown weary, turns to sweet,
And envy, purged by longing, pity is.

And pillows rest beneath the withering cheek,
And hands are laid the battered brows above,
And he whom we had hated, waxen weak,
First in his weakness learns a little love.

XXV

TO POETS

WE are the homeless, even as you,
Who hope and never can begin.
Our hearts are wounded through and through
Like yours, but our hearts bleed within.
We too make music, but our tones
'Scape not the barrier of our bones.

We have no comeliness like you.
We toil, unlovely, and we spin.
We start, return: we wind, undo:
We hope, we err, we strive, we sin,
We love: your love's not greater, but
The lips of our love's might stay shut.

We have the evil spirits too
That shake our soul with battle-din.
But we have an eviller spirit than you,
We have a dumb spirit within:
The exceeding bitter agony
But not the exceeding bitter cry.

September 1914

XXVI

If I have suffered pain
It is because I would.
I willed it.   'Tis no good
To murmur or complain.
I have not served the law
That keeps the earth so fair
And gives her clothes to wear,
Raiment of joy and awe.

For all, that bow to bless
That law, shall sure abide.
But man shall not abide,
And hence his gloriousness.
Lo, evening earth doth lie
All-beauteous and all peace.
Man only does not cease
From striving and from cry.

Sun sets in peace: and soon
The moon will shower her peace.
O law-abiding moon,
You hold your peace in fee!
Man, leastways, will not be
Down-bounden to these laws.
Man's spirit sees no cause
To serve such laws as these.

There yet are many seas
For man to wander in.
He yet must find out sin,
If aught of pleasance there
Remain for him to store,
His rovings to increase,
In quest of many a shore
Forbidden still to fare.

Peace sleeps the earth upon,
And sweet peace on the hill.
The waves that whimper still
At their long law-serving
(O flowing sad complaint!)
Come on and are back drawn.
Man only owns no king,
Man only is not faint.

You see, the earth is bound.
You see, the man is free.
For glorious liberty
He suffers and would die.
Grudge not then suffering
Or chastisemental cry.
O let his pain abound,
Earth's truant and earth's king!

XXVII

WHOM THEREFORE WE IGNORANTLY WORSHIP

THESE things are silent. Though it may be told
Of luminous deeds that lighten land and sea,
Strong sounding actions with broad minstrelsy
Of praise, strange hazards and adventures bold,
We hold to the old things that grow not old:
Blind, patient, hungry, hopeless (without fee
Of all our hunger and unhope are we),
To the first ultimate instinct, to God we hold.

They flicker, glitter, flicker. But we bide,
We, the blind weavers of an intense fate,
Asking but this—that we may be denied:
Desiring only desire insatiate,
Unheard, unnamed, unnoticed, crucified
To our unutterable faith, we wait.

September 1914

XXVIII

DEUS LOQUITUR

THAT'S what I am: a thing of no desire,
With no path to discover and no plea
To offer up, so be my altar fire
May burn before the hearth continuously,
To be
For wayward men a steadfast light to see.

They know me in the morning of their days,
But ere noontide forsake me, to discern
New lore and hear new riddles. But moonrays
Bring them back footsore, humble, bent, a-burn
To turn
And warm them by my fire which they did spurn.

They flock together like tired birds. "We sought
Full many stars in many skies to see,
But ever knowledge disappointment brought.
Thy light alone, Lord, burneth steadfastly."
Ah me!
Then it is I who fain would wayward be.

XXIX

EXPECTANS EXPECTAVI

From morn to midnight, all day through,
I laugh and play as others do,
I sin and chatter, just the same
As others with a different name.

And all year long upon the stage
I dance and tumble and do rage
So vehemently, I scarcely see
The inner and eternal me.

I have a temple I do not
Visit, a heart I have forgot,
A self that I have never met,
A secret shrine—and yet, and yet

This sanctuary of my soul
Unwitting I keep white and whole,
Unlatched and lit, if Thou should'st care
To enter or to tarry there.

With parted lips and outstretched hands
And listening ears Thy servant stands,
Call Thou early, call Thou late,
To Thy great service dedicate.

May 1915

OF WAR AND DEATH

XXX

ALL the hills and vales along
Earth is bursting into song,
And the singers are the chaps
Who are going to die perhaps.
   O sing, marching men,
    Till the valleys ring again.
    Give your gladness to earth's keeping,
    So be glad, when you are sleeping.

Cast away regret and rue,
Think what you are marching to.
Little live, great pass.
Jesus Christ and Barabbas
Were found the same day.
This died, that went his way.
   So sing with joyful breath,
    For why, you are going to death.
    Teeming earth will surely store
    All the gladness that you pour.

Earth that never doubts nor fears,
Earth that knows of death, not tears,
Earth that bore with joyful ease
Hemlock for Socrates,
Earth that blossomed and was glad
'Neath the cross that Christ had,
Shall rejoice and blossom too
When the bullet reaches you.
  Wherefore, men marching
  On the road to death, sing!
  Pour your gladness on earth's head,
  So be merry, so be dead.

From the hills and valleys earth
Shouts back the sound of mirth,
Tramp of feet and lilt of song
Ringing all the road along.
All the music of their going,
Ringing swinging glad song-throwing,
Earth will echo still, when foot
Lies numb and voice mute.
  On, marching men, on
  To the gates of death with song.
  Sow your gladness for earth's reaping,
  So you may be glad, though sleeping.
  Strew your gladness on earth's bed,
  So be merry, so be dead.

XXXI

TO GERMANY

You are blind like us. Your hurt no man designed,
And no man claimed the conquest of your land.
But gropers both through fields of thought confined
We stumble and we do not understand.
You only saw your future bigly planned,
And we, the tapering paths of our own mind,
And in each other's dearest ways we stand,
And hiss and hate. And the blind fight the blind.

When it is peace, then we may view again
With new-won eyes each other's truer form
And wonder. Grown more loving-kind and warm
We'll grasp firm hands and laugh at the old pain,
When it is peace. But until peace, the storm
The darkness and the thunder and the rain.

XXXII

A HUNDRED thousand million mites we go
Wheeling and tacking o'er the eternal plain,
Some black with death—and some are white with
    woe.
Who sent us forth? Who takes us home again?

And there is sound of hymns of praise—to whom?
And curses—on whom curses?—snap the air.
And there is hope goes hand in hand with gloom,
And blood and indignation and despair.

And there is murmuring of the multitude
And blindness and great blindness, until some
Step forth and challenge blind Vicissitude
Who tramples on them: so that fewer come.

And nations, ankle-deep in love or hate,
Throw darts or kisses all the unwitting hour
Beside the ominous unseen tide of fate;
And there is emptiness and drink and power.

And some are mounted on swift steeds of thought
And some drag sluggish feet of stable toil.
Yet all, as though they furiously sought,
Twist turn and tussle, close and cling and coil.

A hundred thousand million mites we sway
Writhing and tossing on the eternal plain,
Some black with death—but most are bright with
    Day!
Who sent us forth?   Who brings us home again?

September 1914

XXXIII

TWO SONNETS

I

Saints have adored the lofty soul of you.
Poets have whitened at your high renown.
We stand among the many millions who
Do hourly wait to pass your pathway down.
You, so familiar, once were strange: we tried
To live as of your presence unaware.
But now in every road on every side
We see your straight and steadfast signpost there.

I think it like that signpost in my land,
Hoary and tall, which pointed me to go
Upward, into the hills, on the right hand,
Where the mists swim and the winds shriek and
    blow,
A homeless land and friendless, but a land
I did not know and that I wished to know.

Such, such is Death: no triumph: no defeat:
Only an empty pail, a slate rubbed clean,
A merciful putting away of what has been.

And this we know: Death is not Life effete,
Life crushed, the broken pail. We who have seen
So marvellous things know well the end not yet.

Victor and vanquished are a-one in death:
Coward and brave: friend, foe. Ghosts do not say
"Come, what was your record when you drew
     breath?"
But a big blot has hid each yesterday
So poor, so manifestly incomplete.
And your bright Promise, withered long and sped,
Is touched, stirs, rises, opens and grows sweet
And blossoms and is you, when you are dead.

12 *June* 1915

XXXIV

WHEN you see millions of the mouthless dead
Across your dreams in pale battalions go,
Say not soft things as other men have said,
That you'll remember. For you need not so.
Give them not praise. For, deaf, how should they
    know
It is not curses heaped on each gashed head?
Nor tears. Their blind eyes see not your tears flow.
Nor honour. It is easy to be dead.
Say only this, "They are dead." Then add thereto,
"Yet many a better one has died before."
Then, scanning all the o'ercrowded mass, should you
Perceive one face that you loved heretofore,
It is a spook. None wears the face you knew.
Great death has made all his for evermore.

XXXV

THERE is such change in all those fields,
Such motion rhythmic, ordered, free,
Where ever-glancing summer yields
Birth, fragrance, sunlight, immanency,
To make us view our rights of birth.
What shall we do?   How shall we die?
We, captives of a roaming earth,
'Mid shades that life and light deny.
Blank summer's surfeit heaves in mist;
Dumb earth basks dewy-washed; while still
We whom Intelligence has kissed
Do make us shackles of our will.
And yet I know in each loud brain,
Round-clamped with laws and learning so,
Is madness more and lust of strain
Than earth's jerked godlings e'er can know.
The false Delilah of our brain
Has set us round the millstone going.
O lust of roving! lust of pain!
Our hair will not be long in growing.
Like blinded Samson round we go.
We hear the grindstone groan and cry.
Yet we are kings, we know, we know.
What shall we do?   How shall we die?

Take but our pauper's gift of birth,
O let us from the grindstone free!
And tre d the maddening gladdening earth
In strength close-braced with purity.
The earth is old; we ever new.
Our eyes should see no other sense
Than this, eternally to DO—
Our joy, our task, our recompense;
Up unexploréd mountains move,
Track tireless through great wastes afar,
Nor slumber in the arms of love,
Nor tremble on the brink of war;
Make Beauty and make Rest give place,
Mock Prudence loud—and she is gone,
Smite Satisfaction on the face
And tread the ghost of Ease upon.
Light-lipped and singing press we hard
Over old earth which now is worn,
Triumphant, buffeted and scarred,
By billows howled at, tempest-torn,
Toward blue horizons far away
(Which do not give the rest we need,
But some long strife, more than this play,
Some task that will be stern indeed)—
We ever new, we ever young,
We happy creatures of a day!
What will the gods say, seeing us strung
As nobly and as taut as they?

XXXVI

I HAVE not brought my Odyssey
With me here across the sea;
But you'll remember, when I say
How, when they went down Sparta way,
To sandy Sparta, long ere dawn
Horses were harnessed, rations drawn,
Equipment polished sparkling bright,
And breakfasts swallowed (as the white
Of Eastern heavens turned to gold)—
The dogs barked, swift farewells were told.
The sun springs up, the horses neigh,
Crackles the whip thrice—then away!
From sun-go-up to sun-go-down
All day across the sandy down
The gallant horses galloped, till
The wind across the downs more chill
Blew, the sun sank and all the road
Was darkened, that it only showed
Right at the end the town's red light
And twilight glimmering into night.

The horses never slackened till
They reached the doorway and stood still.
Then came the knock, the unlading; then
The honey-sweet converse of men,

The splendid bath, the change of dress,
Then—O the grandeur of their Mess,
The henchmen, the prim stewardess!
And O the breaking of old ground,
The tales, after the port went round!
(The wondrous wiles of old Odysseus,
Old Agamemnon and his misuse
Of his command, and that young chit
Paris—who didn't care a bit
For Helen—only to annoy her
He did it really, κ.τ.λ.)

But soon they led amidst the din
The honey-sweet ἀοιδὸς in,
Whose eyes were blind, whose soul had sight,
Who knew the fame of men in fight—
Bard of white hair and trembling foot,
Who sang whatever God might put
Into his heart.
        And there he sung,
Those war-worn veterans among,
Tales of great war and strong hearts wrung,
Of clash of arms, of council's brawl,
Of beauty that must early fall,
Of battle hate and battle joy
By the old windy walls of Troy.
They felt that they were unreal then,
Visions and shadow-forms, not men.
But those the Bard did sing and say
(Some were their comrades, some were they)

Took shape and loomed and strengthened more
Greatly than they had guessed of yore.

And now the fight begins again,
The old war-joy, the old war-pain.
Sons of one school across the sea
We have no fear to fight—

*   *   *   *   *   *

And soon, O soon, I do not doubt it,
With the body or without it,
We shall all come tumbling down
To our old wrinkled red-capped town.
Perhaps the road up Ilsley way,
The old ridge-track, will be my way.
High up among the sheep and sky,
Look down on Wantage, passing by,
And see the smoke from Swindon town:
And then full left at Liddington,
Where the four winds of heaven meet
The earth-blest traveller to greet.
And then my face is toward the south,
There is a singing on my mouth:
Away to rightward I descry
My Barbury ensconced in sky,
Far underneath the Ogbourne twins,
And at my feet the thyme and whins,
The grasses with their little crowns
Of gold, the lovely Aldbourne downs,
And that old signpost (well I knew
That crazy signpost, arms askew,

Old mother of the four grass ways).
And then my mouth is dumb with praise,
For, past the wood and chalkpit tiny,
A glimpse of Marlborough ἐρατεινή!
So I descend beneath the rail
To warmth and welcome and wassail.

     *   *   *   *   *   *

This from the battered trenches—rough,
Jingling and tedious enough.
And so I sign myself to you:
One, who some crooked pathways knew
Round Bedwyn: who could scarcely leave
The Downs on a December eve:
Was at his happiest in shorts,
And got—not many good reports!
Small skill of rhyming in his hand—
But you'll forgive—you'll understand.

12 *July* 1915

XXXVII

IN MEMORIAM

S.C.W., V.C.

THERE is no fitter end than this.
　　No need is now to yearn nor sigh.
We know the glory that is his,
　　A glory that can never die.

Surely we knew it long before,
　　Knew all along that he was made
For a swift radiant morning, for
　　A sacrificing swift night-shade.

8 September 1915

XXXVIII

BEHIND THE LINES

WE are now at the end of a few days' rest, a kilometre behind the lines. Except for the farmyard noises (new style) it might almost be the little village that first took us to its arms six weeks ago. It has been a fine day, following on a day's rain, so that the earth smells like spring. I have just managed to break off a long conversation with the farmer in charge, a tall thin stooping man with sad eyes, in trouble about his land: les Anglais stole his peas, trod down his corn and robbed his young potatoes: he told it as a father telling of infanticide. There may have been fifteen francs' worth of damage done; he will never get compensation out of those shifty Belgian burgomasters; but it was not exactly the fifteen francs but the invasion of the soil that had been his for forty years, in which the weather was his only enemy, that gave him a kind of Niobe's dignity to his complaint.

Meanwhile there is the usual evening sluggishness. Close by, a quickfirer is pounding away its allowance of a dozen shells a day. It is like a cow coughing. Eastward there begins a sound (all

sounds begin at sundown and continue inter-
mittently till midnight, reaching their zenith at
about 9 p.m. and then dying away as sleepiness
claims their masters)—a sound like a motor-cycle
race—thousands of motor-cycles tearing round and
round a track, with cut-outs out: it is really a pair
of machine guns firing. And now one sound awakens
another. The old cow coughing has started the
motor-bykes: and now at intervals of a few minutes
come express trains in our direction: you can hear
them rushing toward us; they pass going straight
for the town behind us: and you hear them begin
to slow down as they reach the town: they will
soon stop: but no, every time, just before they
reach it, is a tremendous railway accident. At least,
it must be a railway accident, there is so much
noise, and you can see the dust that the wreckage
scatters. Sometimes the train behind comes very
close, but it too smashes on the wreckage of its
forerunners. A tremendous cloud of dust, and then
the groans. So many trains and accidents start the
cow coughing again: only another cow this time,
somewhere behind us, a tremendous-sized cow,
θαυμάσιον ὅσον, with awful whooping-cough. It
must be a buffalo: this cough must burst its
sides. And now someone starts sliding down the
stairs on a tin tray, to soften the heart of the cow,
make it laugh and cure its cough. The din he makes
is appalling. He is beating the tray with a broom
now, every two minutes a stroke: he has certainly

87

stopped the cow by this time, probably killed it. He will leave off soon (thanks to the "shell tragedy"): we know he can't last.

It is now almost dark: come out and see the fireworks. While waiting for them to begin you can notice how pale and white the corn is in the summer twilight: no wonder with all this whooping-cough about. And the motor-cycles: notice how all these races have at least a hundred entries: there is never a single cycle going. And why are there no birds coming back to roost? Where is the lark? I haven't heard him all to-day. He must have got whooping-cough as well, or be staying at home through fear of the cow. I think it will rain to-morrow, but there have been no swallows circling low, stroking their breasts on the full ears of corn. Anyhow, it is night now, but the circus does not close till twelve. Look! there is the first of them! The fireworks are beginning. Red flares shooting up high into the night, or skimming low over the ground, like the swallows that are not: and rockets bursting into stars. See how they illumine that patch of ground a mile in front. See it, it is deadly pale in their searching light: ghastly, I think, and featureless except for two big lines of eyebrows ashy white, parallel along it, raised a little from its surface. Eyebrows. Where are the eyes? Hush, there are no eyes. What those shooting flares illumine is a mole. A long thin mole. Burrowing by day, and shoving a timorous enquiring snout above the ground by night. Look, did you see it? No, you cannot see it from here. But were you a good deal nearer, you would see behind that snout a long and endless row of sharp shining teeth. The rockets catch the light from these teeth and the teeth glitter: they are silently removed from the poison-spitting gums of the mole. For the mole's gums spit fire and, they say, send something more concrete than fire darting into the night. Even when its teeth are off. But you cannot see all this from here: you can only see the rockets and then for a moment the pale ground beneath. But it is quite dark now.

And now for the fun of the fair! You will hear soon the riding-master crack his whip—why, there it is. Listen, a thousand whips are cracking, whipping the horses round the ring. At last! The fun of the circus is begun. For the motor-cycle team race has started off again: and the whips are cracking all: and the waresman starts again, beating his loud tin tray to attract the customers: and the cows in the cattle-show start coughing, coughing: and the firework display is at its best: and the circus specials come one after another bearing the merry-makers back to town, all to the inevitable crash, the inevitable accident. It can't last long: these accidents are so frequent, they'll all get soon killed off, I hope. Yes, it is diminishing. The train service is cancelled (and time too): the cows have stopped coughing: and the cycle race is done. Only the kids who have bought new whips at the fair continue to crack them: and unused rockets that lie about the ground are still sent up occasionally. But now the children are being driven off to bed: only an occasional whip-crack now (perhaps the child is now the sufferer): and the tired showmen going over the ground pick up the rocket-sticks and dead flares. At least I suppose this is what must be happening: for occasionally they still find one that has not gone off and send it up out of mere perversity. Else what silence!

It must be midnight now. Yes, it is midnight. But before you go to bed, bend down, put your ear against the ground. What do you hear? "I hear an endless tapping and a tramping to and fro: both are muffled: but they come from everywhere. Tap, tap, tap: pick, pick, pick: tra-mp, tra-mp, tra-mp." So you see the circus-goers are not all gone to sleep. There is noise coming from the womb of earth, noise of men who tap and mine and dig and pass to and fro on their watch. What you have seen is the foam and froth of war: but underground is labour and throbbing and long watch. Which will one day bear their fruit. They will set the circus on fire. Then what pandemonium! Let us hope it will not be to-morrow!

15 *July* 1915

ILLUSTRATIONS IN PROSE

I

RICHARD JEFFERIES (p. 15)

I AM sweatily struggling to the end of *Faust II*, where Goethe's just showing off his knowledge. I am also reading a very interesting book on Goethe and Schiller; very adoring it is, but it lets out quite unconsciously the terrible dryness of their entirely intellectual friendship and (Goethe's at least) entirely intellectual life. If Goethe really died saying "more light," it was very silly of him: what *he* wanted was more warmth. G. and S. apparently made friends, on their own confession, merely because their ideas and artistic ideals were the same, which fact ought to be the very first to make them bore one another.

All this is leading to the following conclusion. The Germans can act Shakespeare, have good beer and poetry, but their prose is cobwebby stuff. Hence I want to read some good prose again. Also it is summer. And for a year or two I had always laid up "The Pageant of Summer" as a treat for a hot July. In spite of all former vows of celibacy in the way of English, now's the time. So, unless the cost of book-postage here is ruinous, could you send me a small volume of Essays by Richard Jefferies called *The Life of the Fields*, the first essay in the series being the Pageant of Summer? No particular hurry, but I should be amazingly grateful if you'll send it (it's quite a little book), especially as I presume the pageant of summer takes place in that part of the country where I should be now had —— had a stronger will than you. In the midst of my setting up and smashing of deities—Masefield, Hardy, Goethe—I always fall back on Richard Jefferies wandering about in the background. I have at least the tie of locality with him. (*July* 1914)

I've given up German prose altogether. It's like a stale cake compounded of foreign elements. So I have laid in a huge store of Richard Jefferies for the rest of July, and read him none the less voraciously because we are countrymen. (I know it's wrong of me, but I count myself as Wiltshire....) When I die (in sixty years) I am going to leave all my presumably enormous fortune to Marlborough on condition that a thorough knowledge of Richard Jefferies is ensured by the teaching there. I think it is only right considering we are bred upon the self-same hill. It would also encourage Naturalists and discourage cricketers....

But, in any case, I'm not reading so much German as I did ought to. I dabble in their modern poetry, which is mostly of the morbidly religious kind. The language is massively beautiful, the thought is rich and sleek, the air that of the inside of a church. Magnificent artists they are,

with no inspiration, who take religion up as a very
responsive subject for art, and mould it in their
hands like sticky putty.   There are magnificent
parts in it, but you can imagine what a relief it was
to get back to Jefferies and Liddington Castle.
(*July* 1914)

II

IBSEN (pp. 61, 62)

Ibsen's last, *John Gabriel Borkman*, is a wonderfully fine play, far better than any others by Ibsen
that I have read or seen, but I can imagine it would
lose a good deal in an English translation.   The
acting of the two middle-aged sisters who are the
protagonists was marvellous.   The men were a good
deal more difficult to hear, but also very striking.
Next to the fineness of the play (which has far more
poetry in it than any others of his I've read, though
of course there's a bank in the background, as there
always seems to be in Ibsen)—the apathy of the
very crowded house struck me most.   There was
very little clapping at the end of the acts: at the end
of the play none, which was just as well because
one of them was dead and would have had to jump
up again.   So altogether I am very much struck by
my first German theatre, though the fineness of the
play may have much to do with it.   It was just a
little spoilt by the last Act being in a pine forest on
a hill with sugar that was meant to look like snow.
This rather took away from the effect of the scene,

which in the German is one of the finest things I have ever heard, possessing throughout a wonderful rhythm which may or may not exist in the original. What a beautiful language it can be! (13 *February* 1914)

I have been reading many criticisms of *John Gabriel Borkman*, and it strikes me more and more that it is the most remarkable play I have ever read. It is head and shoulders above the others of Ibsen's I know: a much broader affair. John Gabriel Borkman is a tremendous character. His great desire, which led him to overstep the law for one moment, and of course he was caught and got eight years, was "Menschenglück zu schaffen[1]." One moment Ibsen lets you see one side of his character (the side he himself saw) and you see the Perfect Altruist: the next moment the other side is turned, and you see the Complete Egoist. The play all takes place in the last three hours of J. G. B.'s life, and in these three hours his real love, whom he had rejected for business reasons and married her twin-sister, shows him for the first time the Egoist that masqueraded all its life as Altruist. The technique is perfect and it bristles with minor problems. It is absolutely fair, for if J. G. B. had sacrificed his ideals and married the right twin, he would not have been deserted after his disgrace. And the way that during the three hours the whole past history of the man comes

[1] To bring about human happiness.

out is marvellous. The brief dialogue between the sisters which closes the piece is fine, and suddenly throws a new light on the problem of how the tragedy could have been evaded, when you thought all that could be said had been said. (20 *February* 1914)

I feel that this visit to Schwerin will spoil me for the theatre for the rest of my life. I have never ceased to see *John Gabriel Borkman* mentally since my second visit to it (when the acting was even finer than before and struck me as a perfect presentation of a perfect play). My only regret was that the whole family wasn't there as well. I should so like to talk it over with you, and the way that at the very end of his last play Ibsen sums up the object against which all his battle was directed: "Es war viel mehr die Kälte die ihn tötete." "Die Kälte, sagst du, die Kälte! die hat ihn schon längst getötet."..."Ja, die Herzenskälte[1]." (10 *April* 1914)

[The play] at the Königliches Schauspielhaus[2] [Berlin] was Ibsen's *Peer Gynt* with Grieg's incidental music—the Northern Faust, as it is called: though the mixture of allegory and reality is not carried off so successfully as in the Southern Faust.

---

[1] "It was rather the cold that killed him." "The cold, say you, the cold! Why, that killed him long ago."... "Yes, coldness of heart."

[2] Royal Theatre.

Peer Gynt has the advantage of being a far more human and amiable creature, and not a cold fish like Faust. I suppose that difference is also to be found in the characters of the respective authors. I always wanted to know why Faust had no relations to make demands on him. Peer Gynt is a charmingly light piece, with an irresistible mixture of fantastical poetry and a very racy humour. The scene where Peer returns to his blind and dying mother and, like a practical fellow, instead of sentimentalizing, sits himself on the end of her bed, persuades her it is a chariot and rides her up to heaven, describing the scenes on the way, the surliness of St Peter at the gate, the appearance of God the Father, who "put Peter quite in the shade" and decided to let mother Aasa in, was delightful. The acting was of course perfect. (5 *June* 1914)

III
THE ODYSSEY (p. 81)

The *Odyssey* is a great joy when once you can read it in big chunks and not a hundred lines at a time, being [forced] to note all the silly grammatical strangenesses. I could not read it in better surroundings for the whole tone of the book is so thoroughly German and domestic. A friend of sorts of the ——s died lately; and when the Frau attempted to break the news to Karl at table, he immediately said "Don't tell me anything sad while I'm eating." That very afternoon I came across someone in the

Odyssey who made, under the same circumstances, precisely the same remark[1]. In the *Odyssey* and in Schwerin alike they are perfectly unaffected about their devotion to good food. In both too I find the double patriotism which suffers not a bit from its duplicity—in the *Odyssey* to their little Ithaca as well as to Achaea as a whole; here equally to the Kaiser and the pug-nosed Grand Duke. In both is the habit of longwinded anecdotage in the same rambling irrelevant way, and the quite unquenchable hospitality. And the Helen of the *Odyssey* bustling about a footstool for Telemachus or showing off her new presents (she had just returned from a jaunt to Egypt)—a washing-tub, a spindle, and a work-basket that ran on wheels (think!)—is the perfect German Hausfrau. (*27 March* 1914)

If I had the smallest amount of patience, steadiness or concentrative faculty, I could write a brilliant book comparing life in Ithaca, Sparta and holy Pylos in the time of Odysseus with life in Mecklenburg-Schwerin in the time of Herr Dr ——. In both you get the same unquenchable hospitality and perfectly unquenchable anecdotage faculty. In both whenever you make a visit or go into a house, they are "busying themselves with a meal." Du lieber Karl (I mean Herr Dr ——) has three times, when his wife has tried to talk of death, disease or crime [at] table, unconsciously given a literal trans-

[1] *Odyssey*, IV, 193, 194.

lation of Peisistratus's sound remark οὐ γὰρ ἐγώ
γε τέρπομ' ὀδυρόμενος μεταδόρπιος[1]—and that is
their attitude to meals throughout. Need I add the
ἀγλαὰ δῶρα[2] they insist on giving their guests, with
the opinion that it is the host that is the indebted
party and the possession of a guest confers honour
and responsibility: and their innate patriotism, the
οὔ τοι ἐγώ γε ης γαίης δύναμαι γλυκερώτερον ἄλλο
ἰδέσθαι[3] spirit (however dull it is)—to complete
the parallel? So I am really reading it in sympathetic surroundings, and when I have just got past
the part where Helen shows off to Menelaus her new
work-basket that runs on wheels, and the Frau
rushes in to show me her new water-can with a
spout designed to resemble a pig—I see the two
are made from the same stuff (I mean, of course,
Helen and Frau ——, not Frau —— and the pig).
Also, I enjoy being able to share in a quiet amateur
way with Odysseus his feelings about "were it but
the smoke leaping up from his own land." (23 *April*
1914)

Good luck to Helen of Troy. As you say, she
loved her own sex as well. Her last appearance in
Homer is when Telemachus was just leaving her
and Menelaus after paying them a visit in Sparta,
"and she stood on the doorstep with a robe in her

---

[1] I do not like having to lament during supper.—
Odyssey, IV, 193, 194.   [2] Splendid gifts.
[3] I for my part can see nothing sweeter than one's own
country.—*Odyssey*, IX, 27, 28.

hand and spoke a word and called him, 'I also am giving thee a gift, dear child,—this, a memorial of Helen's handiwork, against the day of thy marriage to which we all look forward, that thou mayest give it to thy wife: till then, let it be stored in thy palace under thy mother's care.'" But she never gives to me the impression in Homer of being quite happy. I'm sure she was always dull down in Sparta with fatherly old Menelaus—though she never showed it of course. But there is always something a little wistful in her way of speaking. She only made other people happy and consequently another set of other people miserable. One of the best things in the *Iliad* is the way you are made to feel (without any statement) that Helen fell really in love with Hector —and this shows her good taste, for of all the Homeric heroes Hector is the only unselfish man. She seems to me only to have loved to please Menelaus and Paris but to have really loved Hector —and naturally, for Hector and Achilles, the altruist and the egoist, were miles nobler than any one else on either side—but Hector never gave any sign that he regarded her as anything more than his distressed sister-in-law. But after Hector's death she must have left part of her behind her, and made a real nice wife to poor pompous Menelaus in his old age. She seems to have had a marvellous power of adaptability. (*April* 1914)

I made my pilgrimage on Saturday, when, though

I had to get up with the lark to hear the energetic old Eucken lecture at 7 a.m., I had no lecture after 10, and went straight off to Weimar. I spent the rest of the morning (actually) in the museum, inspecting chiefly Preller's wall-paintings of the *Odyssey*. They are the best criticism of the book I have seen and gave me a new and more pleasant idea of Odysseus. Weimar does not give the same impression of musty age as parts of Jena. It seems a flourishing well-watered town, and I should like very much to live there, chiefly for the sake of the park. The name "Park" puts one off, but it is really a beautiful place like a college garden on an extensive scale. After I had wandered about there very pleasantly for an hour or so, I noticed a statue in a prominent position above me. "Another Goethe," thought I; but I looked at it again, and it had not that look of self-confident self-conscious greatness that all the Goethes have. So I went up to it and recognised a countryman—looking down from this height on Weimar, with one eye half-closed and an attitude of head expressing amused and tolerant but penetrating interest. It was certainly the first satisfactory representation of Shakespeare I have ever seen. It appears quite new, but I could not discover the sculptor's name. The one-eye-half-closed trick was most effective; you thought "this is a very humorous kindly human gentleman"— then you went round to the other side and saw the open eye! (8 *May* 1914)

IV

GERMANY (p. 73)

In the evening I am generally to be found avoiding a certain insincere type of German student, who hunts me down ostensibly to "tie a bond of good-comradeship," but really to work up facts about what "England" thinks. Such people of undeveloped individuality tell me in return what "wir Deutschen[1]" think, in a touching national spirit, which would have charmed Plato. But they don't charm me. Indeed I see in them the very worst result of 1871. They have no idea beyond the "State," and have put me off Socialism for the rest of my life. They are not the kind of people, as [the Irish R.M.] puts it, "you could borrow half-a-crown to get drunk with." But such is only a small proportion and come from the north and west; they just show how Sedan has ruined one type of German, for I'm sure the German nature is the nicest in the world, as far as it is not warped by the German Empire. I like their lack of reserve and self-consciousness, our two national virtues. They all write poetry and recite it with gusto to any three hours' old acquaintance. We all write poetry too in England, but we write it on the bedroom wash-stand and lock the bedroom door, and disclaim it vehemently in public. (*2 June* 1914)

[1] We Germans.

The two great sins people impute to Germany are that she says that might is right and bullies the little dogs. But I don't think she means that might *qua* might is right, but that confidence of superiority is right, and by superiority she means spiritual superiority. She said to Belgium, "We enlightened thinkers see that it is necessary to the world that all opposition to Deutsche Kultur should be crushed. As citizens of the world you must assist us in our object and assert those higher ideas of world-citizenship which are not bound by treaties. But if you oppose us, we have only one alternative." That, at least, is what the best of them would have said; only the diplomats put it rather more brusquely. She was going on a missionary voyage with all the zest of Faust—

> Er wandle so den Erdentag entlang;
> Wenn Geister spuken, geh' er seinen Gang;
> Im Weiterschreiten find' er Qual und Glück,
> Er, unbefriedigt jeden Augenblick![1]

—and missionaries know no law....

So it seems to me that Germany's only fault (and I think you often commented on it in those you met) is a lack of real insight and sympathy with those who differ from her. We are not fighting a bully, but a bigot. They are a young nation and don't yet see that what they consider is being done for the good of the world may be really being done for self-gratification—like X. who, under pretence

[1] *Faust*, II, 6820–3, translated in the last four lines of verse on p. III.

of informing the form, dropped into the habit of parading his own knowledge. X. incidentally did the form a service by creating great amusement for it, and so is Germany incidentally doing the world a service (though not in the way it meant) by giving them something to live and die for, which no country but Germany had before. If the bigot conquers he will learn in time his mistaken methods (for it is only of the methods and not of the goal of Germany that one can disapprove)—just as the early Christian bigots conquered by bigotry and grew larger in sympathy and tolerance after conquest. I regard the war as one between sisters, between Martha and Mary, the efficient and intolerant against the casual and sympathetic. Each side has a virtue for which it is fighting, and each that virtue's supplementary vice. And I hope that whatever the material result of the conflict, it will purge these two virtues of their vices, and efficiency and tolerance will no longer be incompatible.

But I think that tolerance is the larger virtue of the two, and efficiency must be her servant. So I am quite glad to fight against this rebellious servant. In fact I look at it this way. Suppose my platoon were the world. Then my platoon sergeant would represent efficiency and I would represent tolerance. And I always take the sternest measures to keep my platoon sergeant in check! I fully appreciate the wisdom of the War Office when they put inefficient officers to rule sergeants. Adsit omen.

Now you know what Sorley thinks about it. And do excuse all his gassing. I know I already over-dosed you on those five splendid days between Coblenz and Neumagen. But I've seen the Father-land (I like to call it the Fatherland, for in many families Papa represents efficiency and Mamma tolerance—but don't think I'm W.S.P.U.) so horribly misrepresented that I've been burning to put in my case for them to a sympathetic ear. Wir sind gewiss Hamburger Jungen, as that lieber besoffener Österreicher told us[1]. And so we must stand up for them, even while trying to knock them down. (*October* 1914)

On return to England, by the way, I renewed my acquaintance with Robert Browning. The last line of *Mr Sludge the Medium*—"yet there is something in it, tricks and all"—converted me, and since then I have used no other. I wish we could recall him from the stars and get him to write a Dramatic Idyll or something, giving a soliloquy of the feelings and motives and quick changes of heat and cold that must be going through the poor Kaiser's mind at present. He would really show that impartial sympathy for him, which the British press and public so doltishly deny him, when in talk and comment they deny him even the rights of a human being. R. B. could do it perfectly—or Shakespeare.

[1] To be sure we are Hamburg lads, as that dear old tipsy Austrian told us.

I think the Kaiser not unlike Macbeth, with the military clique in Prussia as his Lady Macbeth, and the court flatterers as the three weird sisters. He'll be a splendid field for dramatists and writers in days to come. (*October* 1914)

It [a magazine article] brought back to me that little crooked old fellow that H. and I met at the fag-end of our hot day's walk as we swung into Neumagen. His little face was lit with a wild uncertain excitement he had not known since 1870, and he advanced towards us waving his stick and yelling at us "Der Krieg ist los, Junge[1]," just as we might be running to watch a football match and he was come to tell us we must hurry up for the game had begun. And then the next night on the platform at Trier, train after train passing crowded with soldiers bound for Metz: varied once or twice by a truck-load of "swarthier alien crews," thin old women like wineskins, with beautiful and piercing faces, and big heavy men and tiny aged-looking children: Italian colonists exiled to their country again. Occasionally one of the men would jump out to fetch a glass of water to relieve their thirst in all that heat and crowding. The heat of the night is worse than the heat of the day, and geistige Getränke were verboten[2]. Then the train would slowly move out into the darkness that led to Metz

---

[1] "The war's begun, lad."
[2] Spirituous drinks were forbidden.

and an exact reproduction of it would steam in and fill its place: and we watched the signal on the southward side of Trier, till the lights should give a jump and the finger drop and let in the train which was to carry us out of that highly-strung and thrilling land.

At Cologne I saw a herd of some thirty American school-marms whom I had assisted to entertain at Eucken's just a fortnight before. I shouted out to them, but they were far too upset to take any notice, but went bobbing into one compartment and out again and into another like people in a cinematograph. Their haste anxiety and topsy-turviness were caused by thoughts of their own safety and escape, and though perfectly natural contrasted so strangely with all the many other signs of haste perturbation and distress that I had seen, which were much quieter and stronger and more full-bodied than that of those Americans, because it was the Vaterland and not the individual that was darting about and looking for the way and was in need: and the silent submissive unquestioning faces of the dark uprooted Italians peering from the squeaking trucks formed a fitting background —Cassandra from the backmost car looking steadily down on Agamemnon as he stepped from his triumphal purple chariot and Clytemnestra offered him her hand. (23 *November* 1914)

It is surprising how very little difference a total change of circumstances and prospects makes in the individual. The German (I know from the 48 hours of the war that I spent there) is radically changed, and until he is sent to the front, his one dream and thought will be how quickest to die for his country. He is able more clearly to see the tremendous issues, and changes accordingly. I don't know whether it is because the English are more phlegmatic or more shortsighted or more egoistic or what, that makes them inwardly and outwardly so far less shaken by the war than at first seemed probable. The German, I am sure, during the period of training "dies daily" until he is allowed to die. We go there with our eyes shut. (28 *November* 1914)

We had a very swinging Christmas—one that makes one realize (in common with other incidents of the war) how near savages we are and how much the stomach (which Nietzsche calls the Father of Melancholy) is also the best procurer of enjoyment. We gave the men a good church (plenty of loud hymns), a good dinner (plenty of beer), and the rest of the day was spent in sleep. I saw then very clearly that whereas for the upper classes Christmas is a spiritual debauch in which one remembers for a day to be generous and cheerful and open-handed, it is only a more or less physical debauch for the poorer classes, who need no reminder, since they are generous and cheerful and open-handed all the year round. One has fairly good chances of observ-

ing the life of the barrack-room, and what a con-
trast to the life of a house in a public school! The
system is roughly the same: the house-master or
platoon-commander entrusts the discipline of his
charge to prefects or corporals, as the case may be.
They never open their mouths in the barrack-room
without the introduction of the unprintable swear-
words and epithets: they have absolutely no
"morality" (in the narrower, generally accepted
sense): yet the public school boy should live among
them to learn a little Christianity: for they are so
extraordinarily nice to one another. They live in
and for the present: we in and for the future. So
they are cheerful and charitable always: and we
often niggardly and unkind and spiteful. In the
gymnasium at Marlborough, how the few clumsy
specimens are ragged and despised and jeered at
by the rest of the squad; in the gymnasium here
you should hear the sounding cheer given to the
man who has tried for eight weeks to make a long-
jump of eight feet and at last by the advice and
assistance of others has succeeded. They seem in-
stinctively to regard a man singly, at his own rate,
by his own standards and possibilities, not in com-
parison with themselves or others: that's why they
are so far ahead of us in their treatment and sizing
up of others.

It's very interesting, what you say about Athens
and Sparta, and England and Germany. Curious,
isn't it, that in old days a nation fought another for

land or money: now we are fighting Germany for her spiritual qualities—thoroughness, and fearlessness of effort, and effacement of the individual. I think that Germany, in spite of her vast bigotry and blindness, is in a kind of way living up to the motto that Goethe left her in the closing words of Faust, before he died.

> Ay, in this thought is my whole life's persistence,
> This is the whole conclusion of the true:
> He only earns his Freedom, owns Existence,
> Who every day must conquer her anew!
> So let him journey through his earthly day,
> Mid hustling spirits, go his self-found way,
> Find torture, bliss, in every forward stride,
> He, every moment still unsatisfied![1]

A very close parallel may be drawn between Faust and present history (with Belgium as Gretchen). And Faust found spiritual salvation in the end! (*27 December* 1914)

V

"MANY A BETTER ONE" (p. 78)

——'s death was a shock. Still, since Achilles' κάτθανε καὶ Πάτροκλος ὅ περ σέο πολλὸν ἀμείνων[2], which should be read at the grave of every corpse in addition to the burial service, no saner and splendider comment on death has been made, especially, as here, where it seemed a cruel waste. (*28 November* 1914)

[1] *Faust*, II, 6944–7, 6820–3.
[2] Died Patroclus too who was a far better man than thou.—*Iliad*, XXI, 107.

VI

"BLANK SUMMER'S SURFEIT" (p. 79)

From the time that the May blossom is scattered
till the first frosts of September, one is always at
one's worst. Summer is stagnating: there is no more
spring (in both senses) anywhere. When the corn
is grown and the autumn seed not yet sown, it has
only to bask in the sun, to fatten and ripen: a
damnable time for man, heaven for the vegetables.
And so I am sunk deep in "Denkfaulheit[1]," trying
to catch in the distant but incessant upper thunder
of the air promise of October rainstorms: long runs
clad only in jersey and shorts over the Marlborough
downs, cloked in rain, as of yore: likewise, in the
aimless toothless grumbling of the guns, promise of
a great advance to come: hailstones and coals of
fire. (*July* 1915)

VII

"ETERNALLY TO DO" (p. 80)

Masefield has founded a new school of poetry and
given a strange example to future poets; and this is
wherein his greatness and originality lies: that he is
a man of action not imagination. For he has one
of the fundamental qualities of a great poet—a
thorough enjoyment of life. He has it in a more pre-
eminent degree than even Browning, perhaps the
stock instance of a poet who was great because he

[1] Mental lethargy.

liked life. Everyone has read the latter's lines about "the wild joys of living, the leaping from rock up to rock." These are splendid lines: but one somehow does not feel that Browning ever leapt from rock up to rock himself. He saw other people doing it, doubtless, and thought it fine. But I don't think he did it himself ever....

Masefield writes that he knows and testifies that he has seen. Throughout his poems there are lines and phrases so instinct with life, that they betoken a man who writes of what he has experienced, not of what he thinks he can imagine: who has braved the storm, who has walked in the hells, who has seen the reality of life: who does not, like Tennyson, shut off the world he has to write about, attempting to imagine shipwrecks from the sofa, or battles in his bed. Compare for instance *Enoch Arden* and *Dauber*. One is a dream: the other, life....

The sower, who reaps not, has found a voice at last—a harsh rough voice, compelling, strong, triumphant. Let us, the reapers where we have not sown, give ear to it. Are they not much better than we? The voice of our poets and men of letters is finely trained and sweet to hear; it teems with sharp saws and rich sentiment: it is a marvel of delicate technique: it pleases, it flatters, it charms, it soothes: it is a living lie. The voice of John Masefield rings rough and ill trained: it tells a story, it leaves the thinking to the reader, it gives him no dessert of sentiment, cut, dried,—and ready made to go to sleep on: it jars, it grates, it makes him wonder; it is full of hope and faith and power and strife and God. Till Mr Masefield came on earth, the poetry of the world had been written by the men who lounged, who looked on. It is sin in a man to write of the world before he has known the world, and the failing of every poet up till now has been that he has written of what he loved to imagine but dared not to experience. But Masefield writes that he knows and testifies that he has seen; with him expression is the fruit of action, the sweat of a body that has passed through the fire.

We stand by the watershed of English poetry; for the vastness and wonder of modern life has demanded that men should know what they write about. Behind us are the poets of imagination; before us are the poets of fact. For Masefield as a poet may be bad or good: I think him good, but you may think him bad: but, good or bad, he has got this quality which no one can deny and few belittle. He is the first of a multitude of coming poets (so I trust and pray) who are men of action before they are men of speech and men of speech because they are men of action. Those whom, because they do not live in our narrow painted groove, we call the Lower Classes, it is they who truly know what life is: so to them let us look for the true expression of life. One has already arisen, and his name is Masefield. We await the coming of others in his train. (*Essay on Masefield*, 3 *November* 1912)

The war is a chasm in time...In a job like this, one lives in times a year ago—and a year hence, alternately. Keine Nachricht[1]. A large amount of organized disorderliness, killing the spirit. A vagueness and a dullness everywhere: an unromantic sitting still 100 yards from Brother Bosch. There's something rotten in the state of something. One feels it but cannot be definite of what. Not even is there the premonition of something big impending: gathering and ready to burst. None of that feeling of confidence, offensiveness, "personal ascendancy," with which the reports so delight our people at home. Mutual helplessness and lassitude, as when two boxers who have battered each other crouch dancing two paces from each other, waiting for the other to hit. Improvised organization, with its red hat, has muddled out romance. It is not the strong god of the Germans—that makes their Prussian Beamter[2] so bloody and their fight against fearful odds so successful. Our organization is like a nasty fat old frowsy cook dressed up in her mistress's clothes: fussy, unpopular, and upstart: trailing the scent of the scullery behind her. In periods of rest we are billeted in a town of sewage farms, mean streets, and starving cats: delightful population: but an air of late June weariness. For Spring again! This is not Hell as I hoped, but Limbo Lake with green growths on the water, full of minnows.

So one lives in a year ago—and a year hence.

[1] No news.   [2] Official.

What are your feet doing, a year hence?...where, while riding in your Kentish lanes, are you riding twelve months hence? I am sometimes in Mexico, selling cloth: or in Russia, doing Lord knows what: in Serbia or the Balkans: in England, never. England remains the dream, the background: at once the memory and the ideal. Sorley is the Gaelic for wanderer. I have had a conventional education: Oxford would have corked it. But this has freed the spirit, glory be. Give me the *Odyssey*, and I return the New Testament to store. Physically as well as spiritually, give me the road.

Only sometimes the horrible question of bread and butter shadows the dream: it has shadowed many, I should think. It must be tackled. But I always seek to avoid the awkward, by postponing it.

You figure in these dreams as the pioneer-sergeant. Perhaps *you* are the Odysseus, I am but one of the dog-like ἑταῖροι[1]...But however that may be, our lives will be πολύπλαγκτοι[2], though our paths may be different. And we will be buried by the sea—

> Timon will make his everlasting mansion
> Upon the beachéd verge of a salt flood,
> Which twice a day with his embosséd froth
> The turbulent surge shall cover.

Details can wait—perhaps for ever. These are the plans. (16 *June* 1915)

[1] Comrades.   [2] Far-roaming.

"THE GRANDEUR OF THEIR MESS" (p. 82)

I am bleached with chalk and grown hairy. And I think exultantly and sweetly of the one or two or three outstandingly admirable meals of my life. One in Yorkshire, in an inn upon the moors, with a fire of logs and ale and tea and every sort of Yorkshire bakery, especially bears me company. And yet another in Mecklenburg-Schwerin (where they are very English) in a farm-house utterly at peace in broad fields sloping to the sea. I remember a tureen of champagne in the middle of the table to which we helped ourselves with ladles! I remember my hunger after three hours' ride over the country: and the fishing-town of Wismar lying like an English town on the sea. In that great old farm-house where I dined at 3 p.m. as the May day began to cool, fruit of sea and of land joined hands together, fish fresh caught and ducks fresh killed: it was a wedding of the elements. It was perhaps the greatest meal I have had ever, for everything we ate had been alive that morning—the champagne was alive yet. We feasted like kings till the sun sank, for it was impossible to overeat. 'Twas Homeric and its memory fills many hungry hours. (5 *October* 1915)

"THE OLD WAR-JOY, THE OLD WAR-PAIN" (p. 83)

This is a little hamlet, smelling pleasantly of manure. I have never felt more restful. We arrived at dawn: white dawn across the plane trees and coming through the fields of rye. After two hours in an oily ship and ten in a grimy train, the "war area" was a haven of relief. These French trains shriek so: there is no sight more desolating than abandoned engines passing up and down the lines, hooting in their loneliness. There is something eerie in a railway by night.

But this is perfect. The other officers have heard the heavy guns and perhaps I shall soon. They make perfect cider in this valley: still, like them. There are clouds of dust along the roads, and in the leaves: but the dust here is native and caressing and pure, not like the dust of Aldershot, gritted and fouled by motors and thousands of feet. 'Tis a very Limbo lake: set between the tireless railways behind and twenty miles in front the fighting. Drink its cider and paddle in its rushy streams: and see if you care whether you die to-morrow. It brings out a new part of oneself, the loiterer, neither scorning nor desiring delights, gliding listlessly through the minutes from meal-time to meal-time, like the stream through the rushes: or stagnant and smooth like their cider, unfathomably gold: beautiful and calm without mental fear. And in four-score hours we will pull up our braces and fight. These hours will have slipt over me, and I shall march hotly to the firing-line, by turn critic, actor, hero, coward, and soldier of fortune: perhaps even for a moment Christian, humble, with "Thy will be done." Then shock, combustion, the emergence of one of these: death or life: and then return to the old rigmarole. I imagine that this, while it may or may not knock about your body, will make very little difference to you otherwise.

A speedy relief from Chatham. There is vibration in the air when you hear "The Battalion will move across the water on......"

The moon won't rise till late, but there is such placid weariness in all the bearing earth, that I must go out to see. I have not been "auf dem Lande[1]" for many years: man muss den Augenblick geniessen[2]. (1 *June* 1915)

Your letter arrived and awoke the now drifting ME to consciousness. I had understood and acquiesced in your silence. The re-creation of that self which one is to a friend is an effort: repaying if it succeeds, but not to be forced. Wherefore, were it not for the dangers dancing attendance on the adjourning type of mind—which a year's military training has not been able to efface from me—I

[1] In the country.
[2] One must enjoy the passing moment.

should not be writing to you now. For it is just after breakfast—and you know what breakfast is: putter to sleep of all mental energy and discontent: charmer, sedative, leveller: maker of Britons. I should wait till after tea when the undiscriminating sun has shown his back—a fine back—on the world, and oneself by the aid of tea has thrown off the mental sleep of heat. But after tea I am on duty. So with bacon in my throat and my brain like a poached egg I will try to do you justice....

I wonder how long it takes the King's Pawn, who so proudly initiates the game of chess, to realize that he is a pawn. Same with us. We are finding out that we play the unimportant if necessary part. At present a dam, untested, whose presence not whose action stops the stream from approaching: and then—a mere handle to steel: dealers of death which we are not allowed to plan. But I have complained enough before of the minion state of the "damned foot." It is something to have no responsibility—an inglorious ease of mind....

Health—and I don't know what ill-health is—invites you so much to smooth and shallow ways: where a happiness may only be found by renouncing the other happiness of which one set out in search. Yet here there is enough to stay the bubbling surface stream. Looking into the future one sees a holocaust somewhere: and at present there is—thank God—enough of "experience" to keep the wits edged (a callous way of putting it, perhaps).

But out in front at night in that no-man's land and long graveyard there is a freedom and a spur. Rustling of the grasses and grave tap-tapping of distant workers: the tension and silence of encounter, when one struggles in the dark for moral victory over the enemy patrol: the wail of the exploded bomb and the animal cries of wounded men. Then death and the horrible thankfulness when one sees that the next man is dead: "We won't have to *carry* him in under fire, thank God; dragging will do": hauling in of the great resistless body in the dark: the smashed head rattling: the relief, the relief that the thing has ceased to groan: that the bullet or bomb that made the man an animal has now made the animal a corpse. One is hardened by now: purged of all false pity: perhaps more selfish than before. The spiritual and the animal get so much more sharply divided in hours of encounter, taking possession of the body by swift turns. (26 *August* 1915)

The chess players are no longer waiting so infernal long between their moves. And the patient pawns are all in movement, hourly expecting further advances—whether to be taken or reach the back lines and be queened. 'Tis sweet, this pawn-being: there are no cares, no doubts: wherefore no regrets. The burden which I am sure is the parent of ill-temper drunkenness and premature old age— to wit, the making up of one's own mind—is lifted from our shoulders. I can now understand the value of dogma, which is the General Commander-in-chief of the mind. I am now beginning to think that free thinkers should give their minds into subjection, for we who have given our actions and volitions into subjection gain such marvellous rest thereby. Only of course it is the subjecting of their powers of will and deed to a wrong master on the part of a great nation that has led Europe into war. Perhaps afterwards I and my likes will again become indiscriminate rebels. For the present we find high relief in making ourselves soldiers. (5 *October* 1915)

X

"PERHAPS THE ROAD UP ILSLEY WAY,
  THE OLD RIDGE-TRACK, WILL BE MY WAY"
(p. 83)

No! When I next come down to Marlborough it shall be an entry worthy of the place and of the enterer. Not in khaki, with gloves and a little cane, with creased trousers from Aldershot—"dyed garments from Bozrah"—but in grey bags, an old coat and a knapsack, coming over the downland from Chiseldon, putting up at the Sun! Then after a night there and a tattered stroll through the High Street, feeling perhaps the minor inconveniences of complete communion with Nature, I should put on a gentlemanly suit and crave admittance at your door, talk old scandal, search old House-books,

swank in Court and sing in Chapel and be a regular
O.M.: retaining always the right on Monday afternoon (it always rains on Mondays in Marlborough)
to sweat round Barbury and Totterdown, what time
you dealt out nasty little oblong unseens to the
Upper VI. This would be my Odyssey. At present
I am too cornered by my uniform for any such
luxuries. (*May* 1915)

There is really very little to say about the life
here. Change of circumstance, I find, means little
compared to change of company. And as one has
gone out and is still with the same officers with
whom one had rubbed shoulders unceasingly for
the last nine months, and of whom one had acquired
that extraordinarily intimate knowledge which
comes of constant συνουσία[1], one does not notice
the change: until one or two or three drop off. And
one wonders why.

They are extraordinarily close, really, these
friendships of circumstance, distinct as they remain
from friendships of choice....Only, I think, once
or twice does one stumble across that person into
whom one fits at once: to whom one can stand
naked, all disclosed. But circumstance provides the
second best: and I'm sure that any gathering of
men will in time lead to a very very close half-
friendship between them all (I only say half-friend-
ship because I wish to distinguish it from the other).

[1] Companionship.

So there has really been no change in coming over here: the change is to come when half of this improvised "band of brothers" are wiped away in a day. We are learning to be soldiers slowly—that is to say, adopting the soldierly attitude of complete disconnection with our job during odd hours. No shop. So when I think I should tell you "something about the trenches," I find I have neither the inclination nor the power.

This however. On our weekly march from the trenches back to our old farmhouse a mile or two behind, we leave the communication-trench for a road, hedged on one side only, with open ploughland to the right. It runs a little down hill till the road branches. Then half left up over open country goes our track, with the ground shelving away to the right of us. Can you see it? The Toll House to the First Post on Trainers Down on a small scale. There is something in the way that at the end of the hedge the road leaps up to the left into the beyond that puts me in mind of Trainers Down. It is what that turn into unhedged country and that leap promises, not what it achieves, that makes the likeness. It is nothing when you get up, no wildness, no openness. But there it remains to cheer me on each relief....

I hear that a *very* select group of public schools will by this time be enjoying the Camp "somewhere in England." May they not take it too seriously! Seein' as 'ow all training is washed out as soon as you turn that narrow street corner at Boulogne, where some watcher with a lantern is always up for the English troops arriving, with a "Bon courage" for every man.

A year ago to-day—but that way madness lies. (4 *August* 1915)

NOTES

P. 3 (I). Barbury Camp is on the northern escarp-
ment of the Marlborough downs, between five and six
miles north by west from Marlborough. The camp on
the summit is of pre-Roman origin. The preference
for rain and windy weather, shown in this and other
poems in the book, has suggested the poem entitled
"Sorley's Weather" by Captain Robert Graves
(*Fairies and Fusiliers*, 1917) which ends with the verse,

> Yet rest there, Shelley, on the sill,
>   For though the winds come frorely
> I'm away to the rain-blown hill
>   And the ghost of Sorley.

P. 6 (II). Printed in *The Marlburian*, 28 July 1913.
In this case, and in a few other cases, the text in the
book varies slightly from that given in *The Marlburian*.
In these variations the author's manuscript has been
followed.

P. 8 (III). *The Marlburian*, 3 December 1913. East
Kennet is a village on the Kennet between four and five
miles west of Marlborough. A correspondent, who is
familiar with the district, thinks that the church seen
by the author from the cornfield was not that of East
Kennet but the neighbouring church of West Overton.

P. 10 (IV). *The Marlburian*, 9 October 1913. This
poem, said the author, in sending a copy of it home
from Germany, "has too much copy from Meredith in
it, but I value it as being (with 'Return') a memorial
of my walk to Marlborough last September" (1913).
The scenery of this walk is recalled in XXXVI (pp. 83,
84). P. 11, line 2: *hedge's, bird's*; the apostrophe was
misplaced in editions 1 to 3.

P. 15 (VI). *The Marlburian*, 9 October 1913. This
poem is a result of the same walk as IV and V. Liddington Castle is about seven miles north by east from

Marlborough and, like Barbury Camp, guards the northern frontier of the downs. Describing a walk three months before, the author wrote, " I then scaled Liddington Castle, which is no more a castle than I am, but a big hill with a fine Roman camp on the top, and a view all down the Vale of the White Horse to the north and the Kennet valley to the south. I sat there for about an hour, reading *Wild Life in a Southern County*, with which I had come armed—the most appropriate place in the world to read it from, as it was on Liddington Castle that Richard Jefferies wrote it and many others of his books, and as it is Jefferies' description of how he saw the country from there." Line 7: *Coate*, a village to the south (now a suburb) of Swindon, and the birthplace of Jefferies.

P. 16 (VII). *The Marlburian*, 9 October 1913. This poem is a lament over the departure of a Marlborough master, the laureate of the school, who had resigned and left Marlborough at the end of the previous summer term. The author's acquaintance with him was entirely an out-of-school one. See note on XXXVI. Line 1: *Granham hill*, on the opposite side of the Kennet from Marlborough College. The *horse* is a rather inferior specimen of the "white horses," cut out in the chalk, of which there are other and more famous examples in the Wiltshire and Berkshire downs. It was cut by boys of a local proprietary school in 1804. Line 3: *Four Miler*, the school name for Four Mile Clump, so called because it lies at the fourth milestone on the old Swindon Road; it is in the same direction as Barbury Camp and about a mile short of it. Line 19: *toun o' touns*, one of several echoes in the poem of J. B.'s school songs "The Scotch Marlburian" and "All Aboard."

P. 17 (VIII). *The Marlburian*, 10 February 1914. Oare Hill is on the north-eastern border of Pewsey Vale between three and four miles from Marlborough

College. West Woods are on the western side of the valley and nearer Marlborough.

P. 26 (x). Line 11: *Clinton Stiles* has not been identified and is probably imaginary.

P. 29 (xi). This poem was sent to a friend in December 1914. The author wrote, "I have tried for long to express in words the impression that the land north of Marlborough must leave.... Simplicity, paucity of words, monotony almost, and mystery are necessary. I think I have got it at last." Sending it home, along with a number of others, in April 1915, he described it as "the last of my Marlborough poems." Line 7: the *signpost*, which figures here as well as elsewhere (pp. 76, 83) in the poems, stands at "the junction of the grass tracks on the Aldbourne [Poulton] downs—to Ogbourne, Marlborough, Mildenhall, and Aldbourne. It stands up quite alone."

P. 33 (xii). *The Marlburian*, 31 October 1912. Line 2: *Court*, the quadrangle, surrounded by classrooms, hall, chapel, and college houses, and intersected by a lime-tree avenue between the gate and C House. This house (to which the author belonged) was the old mansion of the Seymours, built in the middle of the seventeenth century, and is the only ancient part of the college buildings. Line 6: *sweat* (school slang), run. P. 34, line 1: *Four Miler*, see note on vii.

P. 36 (xiii). *The Marlburian*, 11 November 1912. Line 2: *kish* (pronounced *kīsh*), a flat cushion which folds double and is used by the boys as a book-carrier. The "bloods" (or athletic aristocrats of the school) affect garish colours (*loud and gay*) for the lining of their kishes. Line 4: *barnes* (school slang), trousers. The school rules for dress are slightly relaxed for "bloods." Line 11: *forty-cap*, for football, equivalent to about second fifteen—obtained by the author a year after these verses were written.

P. 40 (XIV). *The Marlburian*, 10 July 1913.

P. 45 (XV). *The Marlburian*, 31 October 1912.

P. 48 (XVI). *The Marlburian*, 19 December 1912. The lines

I know that there is beauty where the low streams run,
And the weeping of the willows and the big sunk sun,

are perhaps the only lines in the book which recall the scenery of the author's Cambridge home.

P. 51 (XVII). *The Marlburian*, 25 February 1913. This poem, as there printed, was preceded by the explanation, "Early in January a man, without any conceivable reason for doing so, drowned himself in the ——. The verdict at the inquest was, as is usual in such cases, 'Suicide during temporary insanity.' This is the truth." Line 18: *river*, by mistake printed *river's* in editions 1 to 3.

P. 54 (XVIII). *The Marlburian*, 13 March 1913. Line 15: *the highway and the way*, cp. Isaiah xxxv. 8.

P. 56 (XIX). *The Marlburian*, 10 July 1913. The rookery referred to is evidently that in the Wilderness, lying between C House and the bathing-place, and visible from the author's dormitory window. Underneath the trees in the Wilderness a good deal of rubbish (*rusty iron*, etc.) had been thrown.

P. 57 (XX). *The Marlburian*, 28 July 1913.

Pp. 61, 62 (XXIII, XXIV), entitled in the author's manuscript "Two Songs from Ibsen's Dramatic Poems." They are not translations from Ibsen, but the author's own impressions of the dramatist's characters.

P. 66 (XXVII). This poem had its origin in the author's journey from the Officers' Training Camp at Churn in Berkshire to join his regiment at Shorncliffe on 18 September 1914, when he arrived at Paddington Station shortly before the special train left which took the Marlborough boys back to school for the term. The first draft of the poem was sent to a friend soon afterwards with the words, "Enclosed the poem which eventually came out of the first day of term at Paddington. Not much trace of the origin left; but I think it should get a prize for being the first poem written since August 4th that isn't patriotic." The draft differs in one place from the final form of the poem, and, instead of the present title, it is preceded by the verse, "And these all, having obtained a good report through faith, received not the promise."

P. 68 (XXIX). Printed, after the author's death, in *The Times Literary Supplement*, 28 October 1915.

P. 71 (XXX). There is external evidence, though it is not quite conclusive, for dating this poem in August 1914.

P. 73 (XXXI). There is the same evidence for dating this poem also in August 1914.

P. 76 (XXXIII). A copy of the former of these two sonnets was sent to a friend with the title "Death—and the Downs." The title in the book is taken from the copy sent home by the author.

P. 78 (XXXIV). This sonnet was found in the author's kit sent home from France after his death.

P. 79 (XXXV). This poem was sent to a friend in July 1915. It appeared for the first time in the second edition.

P. 81 (XXXVI). The epistle in verse (fragments of which have been communicated to the editor and are printed here) was sent anonymously to J. B. (see note to VII). He discovered the authorship by sending the envelope of the letter to a Marlborough master, and replied in the beautiful verses which the editor is allowed to quote:

> From far away there comes a Voice,
>   Singing its song across the sea—
> A song to make man's heart rejoice—
>   Of Marlborough and the Odyssey.

A Voice that sings of Now and Then,
　Of minstrel joys and tiny towns,
Of flowering thyme and fighting men,
　Of Sparta's sands and Marlborough's Downs.

God grant, dear Voice, one day again
　We see those Downs in April weather,
And snuff the breeze and smell the rain,
　And stand in C House Porch together.

P. 82, line 11: κ.τ.λ. (*kai ta loipa*), et cetera. Line
13: ἀοιδός (*aoidos*), minstrel. P. 83, line 11: *Ilsley*,
about twenty miles due east of Swindon and on the
northern slope of the Berkshire downs. Line 23: *the
Ogbourne twins*, Ogbourne St George and Ogbourne
St Andrew, villages in the Valley of the Og, about five
and three miles respectively north of Marlborough.
Line 26: *Aldbourne downs*, on the eastern side of the
Og and adjoining the Marlborough downs. P. 84,
line 4: ἐρατεινή (*erateinē*), lovely. Line 11: *Bedwyn*,
Great and Little Bedwyn, about a mile from the south-
eastern corner of Savernake forest and about six miles
from Marlborough.

P. 85 (XXXVII). Printed, after the author's death,
in *The Marlburian*, 24 November 1915. Sidney Clayton
Woodroffe, killed in action at Hooge on 30 July 1915
and awarded a posthumous V.C., was a school con-
temporary of the author.

P. 86 (XXXVIII). This prose description is extracted
from a letter home. The title has been supplied by the
editor. P. 87, line 24: θαυμάσιον ὅσον, wonderfully
great.

P. 111. The lines translated from *Faust* are almost
the only example of verse translation by the author.
Another specimen, which was found in a school note-
book, is a rendering of Horace, *Odes*, I, 24. It is not
likely that he would have printed it himself, but it is
quoted here as an epilogue to these notes.

QUIS DESIDERIO

Check not thy tears, nor be ashamed to sorrow
   For one so dear. Sing us a plaintive song,
O Muse, who from thy sire the lute didst borrow-
   The lute and notes melodious and strong.

So will he wake again from slumber never?
   O, when will Purity, to Justice dear,
Faith unalloyed and Truth unspotted ever,
   When will these virtues ever find his peer?

For him the tears of noble men are flowing,
   But thine, O Virgil, bitterest of all!
Thou prayest God to give him back, not knowing
   He may not, cannot hearken to thy call.

For if thy lyre could move the forests, swelling
   More sweetly than the Thracian bard's of old,
His soul could not revisit its old dwelling;
   For now among the dead he is enrolled

By Mercury, all deaf to supplication,
   Obdurate, gathering all with ruthless rod.
Tis hard; but Patience lightens Tribulation
   When to remove it is denied by God.

PRINTED IN ENGLAND
AT THE CAMBRIDGE UNIVERSITY PRESS
BY J. B. PEACE, M.A.

www.ingramcontent.com/pod-product-compliance
Ingram Content Group UK Ltd.
Pitfield, Milton Keynes, MK11 3LW, UK
UKHW042146280225
455719UK00001B/130

9 781107 651739